COMMUNICATING WITH V.A.L.U.E.S.

BY JAMES YOUNG
WITH JIM MAYFIELD PHD

COMMUNICATING WITH V.A.L.U.E.S.

*A Seamless Process to Improve
Personal and Organizational Effectiveness*

BY JAMES YOUNG
WITH JIM MAYFIELD PHD

———— ❧ ————

TWI Publishing

First Printing, March 2006
Second Printing, March 2010
APPA Edition, August 2012

This book may not be reproduced, in whole or part, by means of photocopying, scanning, duplicating, printing, audio recording, video recording, via distribution on the internet, or by any other means, without written permission of the publisher.

ISBN: 978-0-9842678-1-1

Library of Congress Control Number: 2010923767

Published by:
TWI Publishing
6615 N. Scottsdale Rd., Suite 250
Scottsdale, AZ 85250
TEL: 480-517-1891
Email: info@ethics-twi.org
Website: www.ethics-twi.org

This book is dedicated to our wives Nancy and Shirley.
Thanks not only for your support,
but for filling our lives with love, joy and laughter.

$\mathcal{T}$ABLE OF $\mathcal{C}$ONTENTS

FOREWARD

Community corrections/probation and parole are an integral part of the justice system, critical to the safety and health of communities and American society. The purpose of community corrections is to help restore juvenile and adult offenders to productive lives and to reduce reoffending. The profession has clear and enduring core values. These include a belief that people can change, respect for diversity, and the importance of the professional relationship in enabling change.

Probation and parole officers try to influence offenders to *want to* make changes and to make positive changes in their thinking and behavior. There is clear evidence that it is the quality of the officer-offender relationship that makes a difference with offenders and reduces reoffending.

A community corrections officer must have the key qualities and abilities necessary to develop relationships with people. The officer builds trust and rapport by conveying personal integrity, as well as genuine interest and concern, and a spirit of cooperation and partnership. The officer helps the offender develop goals, identify and resolve obstacles, select manageable action steps, and connect with various resources in the community. Emotional support is provided with an optimistic attitude and expressions of encouragement, recognition, and support.

Community corrections officers will readily identify with *Communicating with V.A.L.U.E.S.* as an effective communication tool. The V.A.L.U.E.S. framework is very applicable to community corrections work and the book provides insights and techniques that officers can use to improve their effectiveness. Chapter 8 by Carl Wicklund will be especially interesting for community corrections professionals and specifically expands on the model's usefulness in community corrections work. Supervisors and managers, too, will find significant benefit in using this model to improve personal and organizational effectiveness.

Barbara Broderick
Chief Probation Officer
Maricopa County, Arizona
Past President,
American Probation and Parole Association

INTRODUCTION

The tap, tap, tap on a nearby wall sounded like beautiful music to Red McDaniel. Imprisoned in the infamous Hanoi Hilton and often in solitary confinement for as long as eighteen months at a time, he was happy for any sort of communication, even taps on a prison wall. Red chronicled his six-year experience as a Vietnam POW in his book *Scars and Stripes* (published by American Defense Institute).

Captured and tortured by the Vietcong, he quickly learned that the greatest torture of all was isolation without the freedom to communicate with other human beings. He observed that if prisoners could not communicate within 30 days of being captured, they started to withdraw and die.

Communication was so essential to their survival that Red and his fellow prisoners designed an acrostic code that they crudely wrote on pieces of toilet paper and then passed to one another during their daily trip to the washroom. The code involved using a certain number of taps to represent letters of the alphabet. It was their only link to sanity.

Communication has been proven time and again to be a key element in successful relationships. A four-year study conducted by the Family Association of America found that the most common problem in marriage was poor communication, occurring twice as often as any other problem.

Ask any employee or employer to name the top three problems they encounter in the workplace, and one of those problems is certain to be poor communication.

Communication can be defined as *"a giving or exchanging of information, messages, et cetera."* Verbal communication can be defined as "who says what to whom with what effect." With these definitions in mind, communication can be considered an art, as well as a science.

Communication includes a message being delivered and a message being received. Problems occur when that message gets changed between the time it is sent and the time it is received. A simple example of this communication distortion is the party game *Telephone*. In this game, a message is passed around the room as one person whispers it to the next, until everyone has had a chance. By the end of the game, the message is never the same.

We know that communication is, at best, complex. And yet, in spite of all the complicating factors, society depends on effective communication. This is true for all relationships—families, friends, students, teachers, young, old, employee and employer.

In the corporate organization, we focus on four areas in which the communication process must function effectively for the company to be most productive and profitable. These areas are leadership, sales and marketing, customer service and coaching. Each area plays a vital role within the organization, as well as externally with current and prospective customers, community leaders and everyone else the organization encounters. Therefore, quality communication is imperative.

Since most organizations have established communication guidelines, the question becomes one of whether or not that communication is effective in moving the organization closer to its goals, and whether or not the communication that is taking place respects the individual in the process.

Rather than focusing on communication guidelines such as computer systems, e-mail composition, or memo writing, the purpose of this book is to explore a basic, simple process that improves the way people communicate. The emphasis of this book is on how people connect, not how they are connected.

It makes good business sense to have a seamless communication process. Consistently using a single personal communication process that is adaptable to leadership, sales, customer service and coaching, as well as throughout the organization, immediately puts everyone on the same page.

Today, more than ever, individuals are coming into the workplace with fewer people skills. Factors such as an increasing emphasis on technology over personal interaction and the erosion of the family structure can negatively impact an individual's social skills. Therefore, it becomes difficult to do their job properly without gaining or sharpening the skills necessary for effective communication.

What if you discovered a communication tool that promised to improve your organization's communication process? What if you could influence the people in your organization to understand one another better, to be more attuned to one another, to respect one another's differences and diversity, and to work together to create synergy? What if you could create a common and practical way to communicate? Effectively employed, *Communicating With V.A.L.U.E.S.* introduces you to a tool that provides the framework for being a successful communicator. The process includes:

V – Valuing
A – Asking
L – Listening
U – Understanding
E – Empowering
S – Serving

This system will not teach you what to say. It will teach you an easier, more comfortable, successful way to make connections that will lead to overall improved communication. Improved communication will open the door for a better exchange of thought.

Our ability and motivation to communicate is a life-long pursuit. Some communication skills are learned by trial and error, some by education and some are inherited through background and culture. All communication is directly affected by our perceptions of our internal and external world. How we perceive ourselves, others around us and our own environment, significantly affects our manner of communication.

The V.A.L.U.E.S. process will give you a simple, effective process of communication. Then, improving performance requires dealing with internal issues. How we perceive ourselves, the industry we work in and how competent we feel in our job are all critical success factors. We'll discuss the power of changing perceptions later in this book.

Embracing a new way of thinking requires a willingness to change. Be deliberate in reviewing your personal communication style as you read—thinking through the way you communicate *on* and *off* the job.

As you go through the V.A.L.U.E.S. process, it is likely to inspire change, and your first reaction might be to resist that change. Resistance is okay and very natural. One of the positive results from implementing V.A.L.U.E.S. is that, ultimately, resistance decreases, and participation increases.

Learning and growing always require change. As in nature, nothing remains the same. Where there is no change in nature, there is no life. In fact, change is the only constant in most organizations today.

Change is good, if it is good change. Resist good change and you miss experiencing the good.

The V.A.L.U.E.S. process facilitates good change. During V.A.L.U.E.S. training, people accept the process with great excitement and enthusiasm because it is simple and fun, and it provides a guideline for forming relationships and creating value. Using V.A.L.U.E.S. during communication gives you *permission* to actually *value* others. And this process allows you to evaluate your effectiveness in personal and professional communication.

On-the-job training usually involves building technical proficiencies. Yet, when it comes to the most powerful skill necessary for success in business today—quality communication—there is little training and virtually no standards. *Communicating With V.A.L.U.E.S.* fills that gap by focusing on effectively applying the process across all organizational functions.

A frequently heard complaint is, "People in *that* department *over there* have no idea what we do or the pressures we face." By using the same V.A.L.U.E.S. process and applying it according to each job function, departments within an organization can better understand their colleagues, leaders are equipped to do a better job of coaching and the benefits continue throughout the organization.

Why would someone working in customer service want to read a section on sales? Because understanding how the process is applied in every area of business helps everyone understand the organization and each other better.

Communicating with V.A.L.U.E.S. brings individuals and organizations together by demonstrating how to improve communication, leading to increased productivity and better understanding. And, of course, better understanding translates into improved internal quality, leading to a more fulfilling work life for the individual and a better bottom line for the organization.

This book proceeds in a very logical manner. Chapter 1 addresses the extremely important subject of valuing people. Chapter 2 focuses on the effective development and use of questions, and introduces a process of forming and asking G.R.E.A.T. Questions®. Chapter 3 examines the skills necessary to be a good listener by exploring the art and science of listening. Chapter 4 examines understanding others and ourselves. Behavior insights using the DISC model are revealed and the importance of defining and improving emotional intelligence. Chapter 5 deals with empowering and empowering others by discovering our strengths and creating a process for meeting your potential. Chapter 6 covers an often-misunderstood concept of serving, including the value we receive from *serving* others. Chapters 7, 8, 9, and 10 provide opportunities for application of the V.A.L.U.E.S. process in the four areas of your organization: leadership, sales, customer service, and coaching. A training curriculum is available for organizations using this process. Chapter 11 provides the conclusion, including a discussion of internal issues of valuing ourselves—critical for successful communication. In Chapter 12, we revisit the key points in each chapter.

We wish you much success as you implement *Communicating With V.A.L.U.E.S.* And we encourage you to try the *V.A.L.U.E.S.* process with the very next person you meet. We think you will be pleasantly surprised at how it improves your ability to effectively communicate.

CHAPTER 1

VALUING PEOPLE

> How much larger your life would be if your self were smaller in it, if you could really look at other people with common curiosity and pleasure. You would begin to be interested in them...You would break out of this tiny and tawdry theater in which your little plot is always being played, and you would find yourself under a freer sky, and in a field of splendid strangers. *C. K. Chesterton*

Fulton J. Sheen, a Roman Catholic bishop, was a television personality for many years. His practical, down-to-earth messages gave help to Catholics and non-Catholics alike. He reported that on one occasion, while visiting an Asian country, he passed by a tattoo parlor and stopped to look at the various tattoos displayed in the shop's window.

One of the samples caught his eye and gave him cause to wonder. The tattoo read, "Born To Lose." Bishop Sheen went inside and asked the tattoo artist why anyone would want a tattoo with those words on his body. The man pointed to his head and replied in broken English, "Tattooed on brain before tattooed on body." Indeed, in order to value others, we must first value ourselves!

Jess Lair, a college professor in Montana and author of I *Ain't Much, Baby, But I'm All I've Got,* wrote about the problem he had with finding value in, and actually valuing, himself. He learned that the first step in truly loving anyone, even ourselves, is to get to know and understand that person's heart. It might be surprising to learn just how many people do not truly know or understand themselves, making it even more difficult for them to know or understand others.

It can be said that we are defined by what we value. Every person has a value system and there is probably something we can learn from one another. Let's take a look at some people who place others' lives at a higher value than their own. Often these people are called heroes. The following true stories are examples of such heroes in action.

A few years ago an airliner crashed into the Potomac River in the dead of winter. A survivor clung to a piece of the plane while waiting to be rescued—the water was frigid and numbing. Every time a rescue line was within his grasp, he passed it to another survivor. Finally, when the others had been rescued and it was his turn, it was too late—he had died from exposure.

There is another story about a man driving to work in Chicago. On his way, he noticed a group of people gathered alongside the Chicago River. He stopped, asked what was going on and was told a young boy had fallen into the river and was struggling in the icy water. It was April and the river was high on the bank. Without another word, the man tore off his coat and plunged into the river to save the boy. It would have been nice if the result of this man's heroics had been good news. Unfortunately, the boy didn't survive and neither did the man who had attempted to rescue him. It was later discovered that the man didn't know how to swim.

Were these two men insane? Thrill seekers, dying to become heroes? Or, maybe these two men were so in touch with the human race that they acted automatically to save members of their extended family—humanity—"without regard for the cost."

The 16th century poet and philosopher John Donne, in his Meditation XVII, *No man is an island*, offers this explanation for why someone might be willing to sacrifice self for the well-being of another, *"All mankind is of one author, and is one volume….No man is an island, entire of itself…any man's death diminishes me, because I am involved in mankind…"*

Heroes come in all shapes, sizes, creeds and colors. We find them in the pages of our history books, and we frequently find them in the pages of our daily newspapers. A Phoenix, Arizona newspaper reported about a three-year-old girl who called 9-1-1 and saved her mother's life. And who hasn't heard about the mother who lifted a car off her small child? Physiologically speaking, she couldn't have performed such a physical feat, but she did, and a number of people witnessed and verified it.

In 1994 a nine-year-old boy named Justin Burns from Mesa, Arizona became an honorary fire fighter. He was honored with this title in front of his elementary school's faculty, staff and student body. When he was five years old, he suffered horrible third-degree burns over most of his body, requiring dozens of operations, and his face remains severely scarred even today. That fateful night four years earlier, he awoke to find his bedroom full of smoke. He got out of the house immediately, but then realized that his family was still inside. In spite of the fire, Justin went back inside the house time after time to rescue his family. The firefighters called him a hero. But Justin simply said, "What I did, I did for my family because I love them. You would do the same thing, wouldn't you?"

Justin had experienced what we all know to be true: what we value enough, we are willing to give our life for. We are committed to what we value. In a crisis, or perhaps even in our everyday life, our actions expose our values.

Some of the best reading material available in our bookstores and libraries is in the biographies of past and present heroes. These books reveal how these people overcame obstacles in their lives, set their sights on higher achievements than their families and peers expected and succeeded where others facing the same circumstances failed.

If history has cited them as being heroes, you can bet that in nearly every case they did some great act for someone else.

There are hundreds of medals awarded for bravery under fire in time of war. For example, Audie Murphy, while still a teenager, was the most decorated hero in World War II. On more than one occasion, he risked his own life to save the lives of his comrades. He became a successful movie star, even playing himself in the movie, *To Hell and Back*. And yet, until the day he died in a tragic airplane accident, he never claimed to be a hero.

Rarely does the *true* hero feel comfortable with the label. Time after time a soldier or marine has declined the hero label, even though they have raced across a battlefield through a barrage of machine gun bullets to carry a fallen buddy back to safety. And time and again, it has been reported that a buddy has crawled through mud and muck, deadly gunfire and the dark of night, to summon a chaplain to administer the last rites to a fallen comrade.

Yes, heroes come in various packages. All of them, each and every one, is involved in mankind, and does not want another's death to diminish him or her. If you study the great men and women of history, those whose reputations have survived, you will discover that the most significant thing about them was their service to mankind. Some of them gained great wealth and power, others left this world with nothing, but what we remember most about them is what they did for mankind.

Albert Einstein was interviewed shortly before his death and was asked if he knew what man's purpose was on earth. The intellectual giant replied, "Yes, I've known for some time now that man's purpose on earth is to serve mankind." Bottom line—the only way we can effectively *serve* mankind, is if we *value* mankind.

Regardless of your personal religious beliefs, certainly one of the great servant-leaders of all time was Jesus Christ. Shortly before his ignoble death by crucifixion, and in response to an argument among his disciples concerning who was the greatest among them and who would hold the highest rank in the coming kingdom, he gave this important lesson to his followers: *"You know that those who are regarded as rulers of the Gentiles lord it over them, and their high officials exercise authority over them. Not so with you. Instead, whoever wants to become great among you must be your servant, and whoever wants to be first must be slave to all."* (NIV-Mark 10:42-44) Then to exemplify this principle, he washed his disciples' feet, even though, traditionally, it was a servant's job to wash his master's feet.

> There is a turnabout you see, it's a chain that sets you free. Recognize that he who leads doesn't always wear a crown. It's hard to wash another's feet unless you're kneeling down.   *Jim Mayfield*

The Pope, the leader of the Roman Catholic Church, has numerous titles bestowed on him. One of these titles is Servus Sevorum Dei—translated from the Latin this means, Servant of the Servants of God. This certainly exemplifies the importance that the Catholic Church places on the role of servant-leader.

Perhaps the simplest way to express this concept is to say, "A true leader is one who values the one he leads by serving him." The **mother** is valuing her children for the purpose of bringing them to the realization of their own potential. The **teacher** is valuing the children he instructs in order for them to develop their intellectual, psychological and social skills. The **doctor** values her patients by helping them overcome the physical ailments that afflict them. The **attorney** values his clients by providing them with legal assistance to protect their constitutional rights. The **minister** values his congregation by helping them to cope with their lives and by providing them with spiritual guidance. The **manager** values her employees by helping them function at their best in their position for the benefit of themselves and the organization. The **salesperson** values the customer or potential customer by discovering what the customer's needs are and meeting those needs with a specific product or service. The **customer service representative** values the customer by making certain he understands the customer's problem, has sufficient authority to solve the problem and meets the customer's expectations with skill and efficiency. The **business coach** values her charges by helping them learn what they need to move forward in their career, or to assist them in overcoming some difficulty in their employment.

The emphasis on all of us, no matter our role, or roles, in society, is valuing others by serving others. That's the way it is, and that's the way it will continue to be, increasing in importance as society becomes more complex and demanding. And we can serve best by deepening our understanding of others, sharpening our communication skills and learning to value people.

Valuing people and providing service where it is needed

yields rewards to the successful server. Those rewards might be overt, such as earning a place in history, or subtler, such as being remembered as one who went about doing well and serving others. Certainly there can be less flattering ways of being remembered!

Consider how much thought you put into how you value others. The value we place on someone is limited only by our ability to see beyond the obvious to the potential each individual has within them. The following allegory can assist in explaining the importance of looking for *potential* value.

There was a creek running right through the middle of a small village. In order to get from one side of the village to the other, the villagers had to cross the creek. But even at its narrowest part, the creek was still too wide to jump. Thankfully, in the middle of the creek was a wide, flat rock. It served as a bridge for the villagers.

One morning, the villagers awoke and discovered that someone had stolen the stepping stone. No one knew where it went, and yet, it seemed that no one really cared. The villagers only knew that they needed another way to cross the creek. So they decided to place some wooden planks across the creek. That solution lasted only a short time, for the planks warped, and the instability of the warped planks made them especially unsafe.

That's why the villagers then decided to construct a footbridge. No one ever thought about what might have happened to the stepping stone. They had their creek-crossing solution, and the stepping stone was forgotten.

Years later, a villager plowing his fields struck something large with his plow blade. Though the farmer didn't know it, he had found the stepping stone. It was probably tossed there years ago when it was stolen from the creek.

The rock was covered with dirt except where the plow had

struck it. At that spot, the rock actually sparkled! The farmer got his wagon, picked up the rock and took it back to his farmhouse. He washed it at the pump and saw how smooth and shiny it was on the bottom. He decided it would make an attractive doorstop. And, sure enough, the farmer's neighbors frequently commented on his stunning doorstop.

Years passed, and the doorstop was passed down from generation to generation. One day, a geologist passing through the village paused to admire the shiny rock that served as a doorstop. He asked the farmer about the rock, but all the current owner could tell him was that it had been their family's doorstop for generations. The geologist asked if he could take a closer look at the rock, and the farmer granted him permission—unaware of what the geologist suspected. As the layers of dirt were rubbed away from the rock, the geologist reported that it appeared the rock was actually a gold nugget! In fact, it turned out that the stepping-stone-turned-doorstop was one of the largest gold nuggets ever discovered in the world!

What was the value of the rock? Was it valuable as a useful stepping stone? Was it valuable as a doorstop and an attractive ornament? Or was it valuable because, once refined, it would be worth a huge fortune?

So it is with people. Everyone has great value. Once you are able to see another person's value, it doesn't take much effort to show them that they are valued. A pleasant greeting can begin the process. A simple hello, a warm handshake, a broad smile or a sincere compliment are all friendly gestures that communicate value and can change a person's day—perhaps even have a lasting impact on their life.

Because these simple gestures of value are so powerful, some healthcare organizations have instituted what they call the *Five-Feet-Ten-Feet Rule.* The rule suggests that when passing someone in the hall at ten feet, you establish eye contact, and at five feet, you verbally greet them. Whether it is a patient, a visitor or a co-worker, the rule gives a tool for valuing others by simply acknowledging the other person's presence.

An assignment used in the Dale Carnegie human relations program instructs the students to go to a busy place such as a shopping mall, walking around with a big smile, looking people in the eye as they pass. Next, the students were instructed to record the number of people who responded to their smile and the number of people who did not respond. A refreshingly large number of test subjects smiled right back.

This practice *might* not be life saving, but then again, it might be the first time that day or perhaps for several days, that the recipient of your smile has had anyone smile at them. A genuine smile, as minor as the gesture might seem, can be the turning point in someone's day or even in their life.

There are other reasons for valuing people. And while some can seem more selfish, they are still good reasons. What you give is what you get—a variation on the Golden Rule. Value others, and they will most likely value you. Value others, feel good about yourself, improve your sense of self-worth and well-being, all while making others feel valued.

PUTTING IT INTO PRACTICE

Yesterday was Sunday, and I decided to fill my day by valuing people. From the morning church service to an afternoon filled with various activities, I spent the day valuing each person I met. The church pastor, the Sunday school teacher, the lady I helped up the stairs, the young child with blue eyes filled with the wonder of his world and the small cactus wren pecking along the sidewalk were all valued people and moments—I even said as much to the bird!

After church, I went to the brunch. I thanked the hostess

and told her how nice she looked. My waitress, though juggling her duties during a busy Sunday lunch hour, still took my order gracefully. I complimented her ability to maintain a calm demeanor in such a busy environment. She chuckled and thanked me, and before I left, she told me that I had made her day, and she wished others could be as nice.

After my meal, I went to a shopping mall. I didn't buy anything. I just went about seeing whom I could value next by offering honest compliments and genuine smiles. And then I made an unplanned visit to a sick friend's home. He was very ill, but his eyes still lit up when he saw me! Later in the day, I called my sister and told her how much I loved her, teased her about the time she broke my transistor radio and told her how much she meant to me as a model for my life. She seemed quite pleased.

Sunday was a good day for me. Valuing people and taking the time to enjoy pleasant moments in the day was refreshing.

There are so many ways to show people we value them— the way we greet them, showing up to a meeting on time and prepared, doing our homework before the sales call, doing the dishes when it is not our turn, remembering a person's name, acknowledging someone for a job well done, asking questions about someone's family or something they are interested in, saying thank you, saying thank you, saying thank you again, trying to understand someone else's point of view, asking questions, listening, making eye contact, remembering another's birthday and using respectful body language. The list is practically endless.

There is a universal principle that never fails: when we value others, we create more value for ourselves.

Dr. Robert Cialdini, author of Influence: *Science and Practice*[1], identifies "reciprocation" as one of the most powerful ways to influence people. He suggests that the principle of

getting back what we give is not only one of the most powerful principles of influence, but mothers teach it to their children in every culture around the world.

People flock to someone who values them in a manner
that leaves them feeling useful and lifted up. These acts of
valuing can declare to the world, "This person is important
and has great value." There is nothing greater you can do.
There is nothing nobler, more powerful or more honoring to
God and the human race than to show others that you value
them through your words and deeds.

In the final chapter of this book, we'll revisit the topic of
valuing; only this time, we'll focus on valuing *you*—emphasiz-
ing ways to develop a better self-image and telling you how to
change self-perception. It is possible to change our lives by
changing our minds. Fine-tuning our perceptions can
improve the way we value ourselves. And the final chapter
also will expand the application of the *Valuing* step of
V.A.L.U.E.S. to organizational functions such as leadership,
sales, customer service and coaching.

CHAPTER 2

ASKING

> Slight errors in the formation of questions result in gross errors in the answers that follow.
> *David R. Hawkins M.D. Ph.D. —*
> *Power Versus Force, Veritas Publishing, 1998*

A defendant was called to the witness stand. The judge instructed him to answer with either *yes* or *no*. The prosecuting attorney then asked the defendant, "Have you stopped beating your wife?" Can you imagine the quandary for the defendant? If he answered *yes*, he was admitting he had beaten his wife. If he answered *no*, then he was admitting to *still* beating his wife. Obviously, the prosecuting attorney was asking a no-win question.

Imagine if a manager asked an employee, "Are you going to quit fouling up your weekly reports?" The employee would be hard-pressed to answer, especially if the manager was not open to the employee answering the question with another question such as, "What do you mean? What am I doing wrong on my report?" The manager might attempt to explain the shortfalls of the report, but considering the kind of question the manager originally posed, any ensuing conversation would probably not be profitable for either of them.

If you ask the wrong questions expecting the right answers, you are probably going to be disappointed with the results. As David Hawkins puts it, *"Slight errors in the formation of questions result in gross errors in the answers that follow."*

In Chapter One, we learned about valuing others. This chapter provides you with an opportunity to improve on a specific valuing technique: asking good questions. By asking the right questions in the best manner possible, you can expect the person to be responsive with feedback that enhances the communication transaction. If you ask the right question in the right manner, it can even inspire the other person to open up—improving the chances for synergy, as well as setting the stage for a better relationship.

Usually, we ask a question because we want an answer from someone else. Sometimes we even ask ourselves a question.

Perhaps the most fascinating thing about a question is that it expects an answer, and in most cases, *demands* an answer. Sometimes there can be no peace of mind until you receive an answer. This is not so surprising, since we are socialized to answer questions when they are asked. We learn that it is rude to ignore a question and that it is only right and proper to answer. "How are you today, young man?" demands some response.

If someone in your office, even someone that you do not like, were to ask, "Is today the 8th or 9th?" My guess is that you would answer them. Right?

In the business environment, questions serve a variety of purposes, and the following list is a sampling of reasons. Perhaps you can add more. Before asking your next question, ask yourself this: "Why am I asking *this* particular question of *this* particular person at *this* particular time?" When you ask yourself *this* question, you are more apt to phrase your question accurately, and in a more focused manner. This will help you to receive an informed answer.

Some Reasons People Ask Questions

1. To get desired information.

2. To pass information to another person.

3. To determine how someone feels about something.

4. To get another person involved in a project.

5. To enhance a relationship with another person.

6. To make another person feel good about themselves.

7. To have another person agree with you about something.

8. To have another person feel good about you.

9. To have another person trust you more.

10. To determine another person's thinking on a given subject.

11. To determine another person's beliefs.

The appropriate question, well phrased, not threatening or insulting, will go a long way toward eliciting the kind of response you desire. Once you have decided why you wish to ask a question, determine what *type* of question you want to ask—a closed-ended question or an open-ended question.

The closed-ended question

The closed-ended question asks for a short answer, many times just a *yes* or *no*. It doesn't ask for - or allow - explanation, discussion or a prolonged response. There are times when the closed-ended question is the right type of question to ask. The following scenarios are examples of its proper use.

- "We're really behind schedule right now, so would you mind working overtime tonight?"

- "Could you have the monthly report done by this Friday afternoon?"

- "Would you mind helping compile some data on this account?"

- "You've been with the company for 22 years, and there are a number of rumors going around that say you're retiring at the end of this year. Are they true?"

The closed-ended question is especially useful if you simply wish to obtain facts from another person such as:

- How many hours of overtime have you put in this month?

- How many kids do you have living at home now, three or four?

- When are you going to move into your new apartment?

- Would you like a Compaq or IBM computer?

- Have you signed up for the department's bowling team yet?

The primary downside of the closed-ended question is that it is *closed*. It does not do much to create interaction. The **manager** cannot use it to discover how an employee really feels about something going on in the company or in his job. She cannot use the closed-ended question to build rapport with the employee. And she cannot use it to gain the trust and confidence of the employee. The **customer service representative** cannot use the closed-ended question to uncover the hostility expressed by the disgruntled customer. The **salesperson** cannot use this kind of question to get to the bottom of the potential customer's reluctance to buy. The

business coach cannot use the closed-ended question to build a relationship of trust and acceptance with the employee.

The open-ended question

In order to enhance the communication transaction and take it from a simple *yes* or *no* response to an interactive success, it is necessary to use the open-ended question. This type of question is used when more than a cursory response is desired. It is useful for eliciting ideas, feelings and thoughts.

The following scenarios are examples of its proper use.

- How do you feel about the company's new insurance program?

- What are some of your concerns about the shift in responsibilities?

- Would you give me some of your feelings, ideas and concerns about opening a branch office?

- Will you fill me in on some of the fun things you did on your vacation?

- What are your thoughts about working with the new computer program?

The possibilities for open-ended questions are limitless. Its usefulness is clear. Open-ended questions are likely to encourage someone to express opinions and concerns, thereby enhancing communication and allowing for better understanding.

Whatever kind of question you choose, make sure it solicits the kind of response you *want* and *need*. Also, make sure it is clear, precise and understandable, and that it is not threatening, insulting or abusive in any way.

Asking the right question is a great way to learn something

you do not already know. One college professor always suggests that his students should not read anything into without first asking a question so that they have something to answer.

You can also ask questions to reaffirm what you already know; thereby, helping you gain an understanding about someone's feelings. You can also use questions to build trusting and workable professional relationships.

It can be said that the essence of intelligence is the ability to ask good questions. The person asking the questions is in control of the communication. In fact, the questions that you ask determine your position in the encounter. For instance, a question such as, "Why can't you ever get…" or, "Don't you ever think before you…" does not communicate the desire to gain any information. Instead, questions like these suggest a desire to demean the other person.

John G. Miller, in his book *QBQ! The Question Behind the Question, What to Really Ask Yourself* [2] says that if we can discipline ourselves to look behind the initial questions that we ask, and consequently ask better questions, then we should get better answers and better results. He links asking questions with personal responsibility. He suggests three simple rules for asking questions.

1. Begin with *what* or *how*, not *why*, *when* or *who*.

2. Use an *"I"* statement, not *they*, *them*, *you* or *we*.

3. Focus on action.

Miller contends that the perfect question is "What can I do?" because it begins with a *what*, includes an *I*, and focuses on *action*.

One system for structuring effective questions is the "G.R.E.A.T. Questions®" technique. Let's review a typical coaching session to suggest how you might use the system.

Assume you are coaching an employee with the hope of seeing an improvement in attitude from this person. After valuing them, putting them at ease and complimenting them on some specific positive performance action they have taken in the recent past, you start with G in the G.R.E.A.T. Questions® technique:

G – General
R – Relevant
E – Expectation
A – Advantage
T – Take-It-To-The-Next-Level

*G*eneral question: How do you feel about the way things are going in your department?
*R*elevant question: How do you feel the overall attitude is in your area?
*E*xpectation question: Do you think this attitude is where we need it to be in order to be most effective?
*A*dvantage question: If the attitudes in your department were where we wanted them to be, what would be the company advantage?
*T*ake-it-to-the-next-level question: Is your attitude where you want it to be?

Another way to handle the situation is to be more direct while still following the G.R.E.A.T. Questions® technique of asking questions.

*G*eneral question: How is your attitude?
*R*elevant question: Why do you feel that way?
*E*xpectation question: What do you feel is expected of you in your present position with the company?
*A*dvantage question: What do you believe will be the

result for the firm if you could meet your expectations? *T*ake-it-to-the-next-level question: Where do we go from here?

Some questions in the business world can be intimidating, disabling, frustrating and even devastating to the person being asked. If a question puts a person on the spot, it can result in defensive or even combative behavior. The following are some examples of this approach.

- What in the world made you do that?
- Why aren't you on schedule like everyone else?
- Don't you know better than to try it that way?
- Doesn't it bother you to lose customers that way?
- When can we expect you to straighten up your act?
- Do you have any idea what people are saying about your performance?
- What's your problem this time?

And then there are effective questions that can become a part of the solution to the problem, rather than contributing to the problem.

- What kind of help can I give you right now?

- How do you feel about the way things are going?

- What kind of results would you like to see?

- What expectations do you have?

- What do you feel is responsible for our success?

- What do you believe is the benefit of doing it that way?

- What two or three things are you most pleased with?

Other questions are those that deal with the now. They should be kept positive and focused on achievement.

- What are some of the good things that happened to you today?

- Can you tell me the two things you learned today?

- What can we finish tomorrow that we didn't get done today?

- What did you do today that you can take pride in?

- What did you do today that helped someone go for it?

Asking effective, thought-provoking questions can move the communication process forward. Keep your questions positive and focused on the issues or problems at hand. Good questions allow, encourage and stimulate good problem-solving answers.

In chapters VII through X, we consider *Asking* as it applies to the positions of leadership, sales, customer service and coaching. These chapters provide more examples of questions that can be used in real-life situations.

Here is an applicable quote from David R. Hawkins on the subject of asking questions, this time from his tremendous book *Power Versus Force:* "Slight errors in the formation of questions result in gross errors in the answers that follow."

CHAPTER 3

LISTENING

> "One person who is truly understanding, who takes the trouble to listen to us as we consider our problems, can change our whole outlook on the world." *Dr. Elton Mayo*

The quality of a person's life can be equated with the quality of their listening. The quality of your relationship with friends, family, co-workers, employer, employees, vendors, customers and clients is largely a matter of how effectively you listen.

Research results show that adults spend about 70% of our waking day involved in the act of communication. Of this time, approximately 16% of it is spent in reading, 9% in writing, 30% in speaking and 45% in listening. With that much time spent listening each day and all the responsibilities placed on everyone in our society to use the information gained from listening, it would seem that our educational system in the United States should provide courses in effective listening.

It turns out that the average twelve-year curriculum in our public schools provides years of training in reading and writing, one or two courses in speaking and not even one course in listening. And yet, listening has been proven to be teachable and can increase a person's ability to listen by a considerable amount.

Perhaps curriculum planners and textbook buyers in our

schools believe that if children have two functioning ears, the skills involved in listening will be picked up by osmosis. It just isn't so. Listening _can_ be learned; in fact, it _has_ to be!

Dr. Ralph G. Nichols, from the University of Minnesota, built undergraduate and graduate programs around the subject of listening because he noted that, generally, people do not know how to listen effectively.

Because so much of an individual's personal and professional success depends on their ability and willingness to listen, it is essential to learn some facts about the listening phase of the communication process. What are some of the barriers to listening? What are the different kinds of listening? What are the reasons why we should learn to be more effective listeners? What is in it for us?

Learning to listen more effectively can, and probably does, affect one's possibilities for advancement and promotion. While creating and asking appropriate _questions_ is important in any role, it is crucial to learn to _listen_ effectively in order to ask the appropriate questions.

Read the following sections carefully, and evaluate your own listening style. Use this material to help you become a better listener. It will pay you to do so.

Some Facts About Listening

Listeners exist so that speakers can deliver a message and get verbal or non-verbal responses.

Every listener has established attitudes and a reason for listening based on past experiences, childhood influences, dreams and educational experiences. The listener brings preconceived notions—some positive and some negative—to the listening experience.

Listeners contribute to a speaker's success or failure. Attentive, involved listeners encourage speakers to continue.

Non-involved listeners can discourage even the most experienced speaker. When a listener's body language communicates apathy, the speaker often loses some of the presentation zing.

Listening is intellectual and emotional. Thinking and feeling always enters into the listening process.

The average listener gets only about 50% of a speaker's message the first time it is heard and loses about 25% of that within two to three days, leaving only a 25% remnant of the speaker's message. Certainly, this is evidence that listener efficiency can improve.

Effective listening takes effort. It is not easy. And yet, we know that effective listeners are more likely to pick up on another person's problems, giving the listener a greater opportunity to contribute to a potential solution.

Failure to listen can contribute to a lack of trust and confidence between listener and speaker, largely due to the fact that all listeners have differing characteristics, experiences, personalities and abilities through which they filter what is being communicated.

Although we know many facts about listening, knowledge alone does not do much to help us put into *practice* what we know. But, it does give us a place to start.

Barriers to Listening

Pretending to listen. In this barrier, the listener appears to be listening, all the while daydreaming or thinking about something more interesting. Sometimes the listener is even looking directly at the speaker, nodding occasionally, smiling as if listening, but in another mental world. Many people practice this technique of listening to the point of becoming proficient!

Considering a speaker's *topic* uninteresting.

There is no doubt that it is difficult to focus and concentrate, that is, *really listen,* when you are disinterested in the subject. If the topic is something that personally affects the listener in a physical, economic or psychological way, the listener is more likely to *really listen.* Personal interests and well-being also influence listening. The key to overcoming this barrier is for the listener's attitude to change toward the subject matter. Otherwise, the listener won't achieve peak listening.

Considering a *speaker* uninteresting. Regardless of the topic, if a listener is disinterested in the speaker, it is unlikely that much of the topic will be retained.

Finding fault with the *speaker*, not the message. Similar to the previous barrier, a listener might also choose to focus on negative thoughts about the speaker. This can include focusing on the speaker's accent, mannerisms, mistakes, stance, grammar or delivery, rather than on the message.

Half-listening or not listening to the whole message. A listener might focus so much on the verbal message—analyzing, criticizing and judging the words spoken—that listening beyond the words to the mood, intensity and heart behind the words can be overlooked.

Being affected by physical distractions. An open window allowing outside noises to come in, a room that is too cold or too hot, cramped or uncomfortable seating or even others in the audience that are engaging in distracting activities such as whispering to an associate, are all examples of physical distractions that can be barriers to listening. It takes focused concentration to overcome these distractions.

Being affected by emotional distractions. Personal trials can cause a listener's mind to wander. Concerns such as an unresolved argument with a friend or family member, a teenager making poor choices, a missed promotion that is long overdue or a loved one diagnosed with a life-threatening disease are a few examples. Psychological distractions can be devastating to a person who might otherwise have had every intention of listening.

Letting personal prejudices interfere with listening. Everyone has personal prejudices about any number of things. Belief systems, values, personal experiences and personal challenges all contribute to prejudicial thinking. It is not a matter of whether or not a listener has prejudices; it is a matter of what one does to control the impulse to let those prejudices interfere with effectively listening to the speaker.

Listening just for the facts, and not the total message. *Bottom-line listeners* simply look for specific information on specific issues. Bottom-liners are only interested in getting the information, not in how the speaker feels or any other extraneous information. Listeners with this approach are going to miss a lot of the message, perhaps the most important part of all, since the speaker might just deliver some of the best material by tucking it in between all the facts and figures.

Spending too much time and thought on organizing. It is the nature of humans to like beauty and order. Wishing to have things in order, or putting things in order, is often the goal of an educated person. It is good to organize the speaker's message as it unfolds. However, organizing can cause the listener to lose touch with the speaker's real message—the total message from the total person. Organizing the speaker's message needs to be tempered with restraint so as not to interfere with the listener-speaker feedback loop that is so critical to ensuring effective communication.

Not allowing for an intellectually challenging experience. Any number of influences can interfere with the listener's ability or willingness to enter intellectually into the presentation. Someone has wisely said, "Learning is painful." When intellectually challenged, a listener either has enough brain capacity to store the information for future reference, or the listener needs to make mental room for the information to be stored. In either case, these responses can cause stress and discomfort. Of, course there is a third response; sometimes it might seem easier to *ignore* the challenging message. Learning can be interesting and exciting—especially when it helps to solve a problem. But, learning can also be characterized as difficult and sometimes even boring. It takes a real commitment to listen to intellectually challenging material.

Though barriers to listening can seem daunting, those barriers can be breached. If you are a listener and find yourself becoming a victim of one or more of the barriers just discussed, do yourself a favor by breaking them down. The first step is to focus on listening. What we focus on, we improve.

Kinds of Listening

Passive listening. Passive listening is really *hearing without involvement,* either physical or psychological. Sometimes passive listening is done just to keep from being rude, but it really doesn't accomplish much. Many speakers are aware that the listening is passive when they observe certain indicators such as a lack of response from the listener. Much of our everyday listening is passive. This is especially so in familiar settings such as in the home, at sporting events, at social gatherings and wherever the payoff for effective listening isn't very high. In other words, when you have no pressing interest at the moment. Sometimes, passive listening occurs only because you happen to be near someone who is speaking, and the sounds travel to your ears.

Active listening. Active listening is when the listener is totally involved in the communication process. This includes physical, intellectual and emotional involvement. In active listening, the listener is physically responsive to the speaker. The listener might sit on the edge of the seat, maintain eye contact with the speaker, nod the head in approval of the speaker's comments, applaud or ask questions, if appropriate. The active listener might also take notes and possibly give feedback after the presentation is concluded. The active listener will undoubtedly receive more out of the message than would the passive listener, and will certainly remember more of what is said. In addition to helping the listener, active listening also helps the speaker, because the listener shows an interest in the message. The show of interest helps the listener to build rapport with the speaker and helps build a bond of trust between the listener and the speaker.

Listening for entertainment. This is an important kind of listening for all of us. On average, Americans spend more than four hours per day watching television, and many people spend quality time listening to music, which takes little effort and is normally quite relaxing. Listening for entertainment also includes listening to talk radio, story telling, eavesdropping and listening to the sounds of nature. Since there is little stress involved, listening for entertainment can add balance to a frantic schedule.

Listening with empathy. Empathetic listening takes active listening to the next level. The empathetic listener pays attention to the words, the emotional intensity and impact of the words, as well as the mood of the speaker, listening for those sounds that come from a place deep down in the speaker. The empathetic listener cares about the person speaking and is willing to join the speaker in the emotional journey the message takes.

Empathy is defined in the American College Dictionary as, "the mental entering into the feeling or spirit of a person or thing." Empathy goes beyond sympathy—feeling sorry for someone in a certain situation. While sympathy is not necessarily bad, it is not nearly as helpful as empathy is in understanding an individual.

An old Native American admonition says, "Don't judge another man until you have walked a mile in his moccasins." This pretty well describes empathy. Walking in another's shoes, the listener is better able to feel the speaker's pain, sorrow, triumphs and joys. Listening with empathy also puts the listener in a position to know how to help guide the speaker, often helping them reach their potential.

Empathy is a marvelous way to come to understand another person. The value of this kind of insight cannot be overstated. However, there are some problems in using this method.

The first, and perhaps the most difficult obstacle, is that it takes time to build empathy. Because of this, some may lose patience. Second, it takes commitment. You have to want to do it. Third, it takes effort. You have to give it your all in order to hear what comes from another person's heart as well as from their mouth. As a tool for understanding another human being, empathy knows no equal. One of the greatest ways to honor and serve another person is to listen empathetically.

Why We Should Learn to Listen

Majority of our communication time. People are more involved in listening than in reading, writing or speaking. This fact alone provides us with a key reason to learn to listen effectively.

Listening to learn. Effective listeners are more inclined to learn. For example, if we questioned ten people we questioned about a particular topic, it is possible that each person would have some knowledge about that topic. And yet, it is also likely that each person's background would significantly influence how that knowledge is processed, making each person's emphasis on the details of the topic slanted or biased. A person who grew up in poverty would have a different view of life than someone reared in relative abundance. Someone raised in a small town would likely have a different view than someone raised in a large city. The challenges and successes each person experiences in life shape the filter through which future experiences pass. This gives our society the richness of diversity of thought that can be so useful for problem solving. The bottom line is that the information others have can be helpful to us if we can just discipline ourselves to listen for learning.

Listening to save time. While it is true that people often fail to listen because they do not feel they have the time, this just might be the furthest from the truth! Very often, effective listening can save you hours in the long run! For example, if a speaker is presenting the findings of years of research on a particular subject, it would behoove the listener to take the time to actually listen. It is easier to check out someone else's facts and figures than it is to start from scratch. Hence the old saying, "Don't reinvent the wheel." It does not mean that one should be gullible or naive. It simply means that since time is so very precious and easy to waste, it is wise to take advantage of every opportunity to learn from others.

Listening to expand one's interest. By listening to teachers, parents, ministers, counselors and peers, children often become so interested in a particular subject that they choose their future careers at an early age. In the same way, effective listening can broaden anyone's base of interests since there is an endless supply of topics and hobbies that can influence one's pursuits.

Listening for influence. Listening can help you win friends and influence people! In studies of why employees like their job, many of them said it was because of the boss they had. "I like my boss, he listens to me." When you listen to others, the law of reciprocity often takes over. This means they, in turn, listen to you.

Listening to build rapport. Listening helps build trust and confidence. Perhaps it sounds odd, but the truth is that the more you listen to others, the more they tend to trust you. And this very often becomes a two-way experience. When they trust you, they listen to *you* more and are more apt to share ideas, thoughts, inspirations and aspirations with each other. In fact, effective listening can build mutual rapport more than anything else one can do.

Listening to become better acquainted. Effective listening can reveal something new about someone. One astute philosopher of the past put it this way, "The greatest study of mankind is man." Really listening to someone else presents a wonderful opportunity to study that person, not in the way that a professional psychologist would study them, but as one human being who is truly interested in another human. An effective listener can learn a deeper understanding of another person, including how to motivate them, how to help them solve their problems and even how to anticipate their needs.

Listening to facilitate career growth. Managers, like anyone else, appreciate it when their employees listen to what they say. And people who listen to their manager are trusted more, are more likely to be given increased responsibility and are more apt to be considered for raises and promotions. Effective listening also helps memory. Knowing more and remembering more demonstrates real value to corporate leadership—therefore, one's career has a better chance to move forward. President Calvin Coolidge, often called "Silent Cal" once wrote, "No one ever listened himself out of a job." Words to ponder!

How To Listen

Before you can practice effective listening, you must consider whether or not the effort necessary for being a good listener is worth the energy needed to get the desired result. This means you must decide, as precisely as possible, just what it is you desire to get out of the listening experience. This can be done by writing down the reasons for listening and what you expect to gain from the speaker and the message.

A very successful technique used by salespeople prior to calling on a client is to anticipate the specific responses— actually talking or mentally walking through the proposed encounter. This includes visualizing walking into the client's office, greeting the client, shaking hands, being asked to sit down, valuing the client, asking some ice-breaking questions, getting down to the presentation, overcoming objections and closing the sale.

The salesperson has, in effect, decided the outcome of the encounter prior to its taking place. Even if things do not go as planned, or even if the speaker does not follow the predicted script, effective listening is more likely to come naturally, and more likely to be rewarded with greater retention as a result of the anticipation and preparation of the listener. Always go into a listening situation with anticipation and expectations.

After considering the desired results, you still must prepare before going into a listening experience. Find out as much as possible about the speaker, and examine any preconceived notions or existing feelings about the speaker. Questions useful during this part of the preparation phase include: What was the last listening experience like with this particular speaker? During any previous encounter did the speaker present his feelings, ideas and position effectively? Do you have any feelings of hostility, dislike or distrust for the speaker?

Is there any fear connected with listening to the speaker? These are just a few of the questions you can ponder when preparing to listen effectively.

Another form of preparation includes researching the topic. Read about the subject before going to the presentation. This method of preparation allows you to evaluate the presentation in light of what you learned before attending. If the presentation is different from what you discovered during your research, you can then listen more carefully to learn if the speaker offers reasons for the difference. If he does not, then the previous research gives you useful information for asking the speaker informed questions at an appropriate time.

You must also decide ahead of time that you won't allow yourself to be distracted by external or internal distractions. This includes clearing your mind before the listening experience begins and eliminating potential disruptions if at all possible, such as incoming phone calls, interruptions by staff members, room temperature, room lighting, refreshments and machine noise. These are just a few examples of potential distractions that can be addressed before the listening experience begins.

During the presentation, you must decide to concentrate and focus on the message. It's easy to slip into daydreaming. An effective listener employs specific strategies for averting prolonged daydreaming. These strategies include specifically listening for the speaker's main point and supporting material, and listening to determine how sub points relate back to the main point. Mentally putting the presentation in an orderly sequence helps you remember more of what is said.

Another strategy for avoiding daydreams during a listening experience is to take notes. Most speakers consider it a compliment when they see someone taking notes. Taking notes communicates that what the speaker says is noteworthy. If, after the presentation, you determine that the notes are not valuable enough for long-term retention, they can be destroyed. Meanwhile, the act of taking notes has most certainly facilitated greater memory retention, even if you don't retain the actual notes.

Remember that the average listener tends to immediately forget 50% of what is heard and 25% more in a couple of days. Taking notes can help recall considerably. A caveat is to keep the note taking from escalating into artistic doodling. In other words, take notes, but don't overdo it.

Next, an effective listener knows to allow the presenter to do most of the talking. Note that we have two ears and one mouth, which can hint on how much listening needs to be done versus how much speaking!

Another helpful suggestion is to use a common brainstorming tool—deferring judgment. Wait until the speaker is finished before making any final decisions concerning the presentation or the speaker. This is critical because often a speaker is using a more roundabout route to get to a conclusion. An effective listener practices patience and waits for the final result. If the effective listener needs to register a disagreement, it can always be done at the conclusion of the message, thereby ensuring that the argument is on more solid ground.

An effective listener also practices empathetic listening. This requires entering into the spirit or feeling of the speaker. It also requires listening to the speaker's words and tone of voice, observing the speaker's body language and zeroing in on every emotion expressed or insinuated. By putting all of this together with what you know about the speaker, you can be confident that the listening experience was the best it could be.

Next, you can use body language to provide feedback, communicating sincere interest to the speaker. By sitting on the edge of your seat, using eye contact with the speaker, nodding in agreement with the speaker, smiling when amused and applauding if appropriate, you are able to offer feedback to the speaker.

The following tools, *Personal Listening Inventory and Self-Evaluation Listening Experience,* are included to help you become a more effective and powerful listener.

Personal Listening Inventory

Complete each of the following statements to the best of your ability:

1. My listening is the *best* when _____

   _____

2. My listening is *less than* the *best* when _____

   _____

3. I listen *best* when I am *with* _____

   _____

4. My listening is *less than the best* when I am *with* _____

   _____

5. Of the listening concepts discussed in this chapter, I am best in:

   a. _____

   b. _____

6. Of the listening concepts discussed in this chapter, I believe I can improve on:

   a._____

   b._____

7. My commitment to becoming a better listener can best be summed up as follows:

   _____

   _____

   _____

   _____

   _____

Self-Evaluation: Listening Experience

The next time you have the opportunity to be the listener in an important transaction (on the job, at home, elsewhere), respond to the following statements:

	Yes	**No**
1. I chose to listen because I wanted to.	____	____
2. I listened because I was required to.	____	____
3. I sincerely tried to listen.	____	____
4. I showed the speaker I was interested.	____	____
5. I let the speaker dominate the conversation.	____	____

	Yes	**No**
6. I understood all the points made by the speaker.	____	____
7. I jumped to conclusions during the message.	____	____
8. I got angry during the presentation.	____	____
9. I prejudged what I heard before the conclusion.	____	____
10. I asked questions, only for clarification.	____	____

Write briefly what transpired during your listening experience, how you felt about the experience, what you learned about the act of listening during the experience and how you would handle the experience if you had the opportunity to repeat it.

_____

_____

_____

_____

_____

_____

CHAPTER 4

UNDERSTANDING

> "It is understanding that gives us an ablility to have peace. When we understand the other fellow's viewpoint, and he understands ours, then we can sit down and work out our differences. *Harry S. Truman*

Yes, well-formulated questions are important. Yes, attentive listening to responses is most important, too. And yet, equally as important is one's ability to understand the responses and the responders in such a manner as to know what to say and do next.

Communication is ultimately a one-to-one transaction. Regardless of one's professional role, the ability to interact with others ultimately defines a person. This is why, without understanding, a listener remains adrift in a sea of words and the one-to-one transaction is incomplete.

The ability to understand what is heard in light of what is known about the speaker is key. And a good place to start gaining understanding is to know the learning style of the person—how the speaker accepts, internalizes, incubates and processes information.

Another facet of an individual's persona is personality style. It is important to approach a person from *their* point of view. In order to successfully counsel, lead, motivate, encourage and respect another person, first seek to know the other person's behavior style. Then, examine how both speaker and listener respond intellectually and emotionally to the messages received. Knowing the behavior style and learning style of the person with whom you're communicating leads to a better overall understanding of the filter through which information is processed.

Learning Styles

Learning is a four-step process. First, you have an experience. Second, you reflect upon that experience. Third, you formulate and ponder scenarios in which the experience can be used. Fourth, you use the experience in new situations. We might call this fourth step the trial phase of learning. And without being fully aware of it, you will repeat these four steps over and over again.

Experience > Reflection > Abstract Creation > New Experiences > Repeat Process

This seems so simple, and yet it is critical to learning. While most experiences come from sensory input and are not necessarily chosen, there are other experiences that can be deliberately chosen. What enters into the latter is that chosen experiences are based on one's own values, beliefs, goals and aspirations. Each person goes about this process with a different level of precision, a different level of risk, a different level of intensity and a different level of commitment.

Some individuals like to operate in this process by having an experience, and then without much reflection or abstraction, plunge into new experiences using what little the first experience has taught them. A good example of this is a child who touches a hot stove. It burns his finger. He says to himself, "I touched the stove on the right side and burned my finger. I think I'll touch it on the left side, and I won't be burned." It might take two or three experiences to teach the youngster that the entire top of the stove is hot and will burn his finger if he touches it. Meanwhile, another child reaches for the stove, feels the uncomfortable heat before touching it, decides after a bit of reflection that the excessive warmth is unpleasant, and withdraws his hand before getting burned. It is unlikely that the child will ever attempt to touch the stove. Another child might touch the stove, get burned, put two and two together and not attempt to touch the stove again.

Sometimes we call these people slow, medium and fast learners. The process is still the same. It is to have an experience, think about the experience, make an abstract decision and act or refrain from acting as a result. It just depends on your learning style as to how that process unfolds.

Learning theorists have identified four learning styles. The four names we have selected are somewhat generic. They are *feelers, thinkers, doer,* and *watchers.*

The *feeler,* like the first child in the preceding example, reaches out and touches the stove without thought of consequences. *Feelers* do what they want to do, when they want to do it, and they learn best by doing it their way. They rely mostly on their intuition—their feelings. This intuition, or feeling, often occurs as a result of experience. They do not rely much on theory. Their research is primarily doing things by trial and error. *Feelers* are comfortable in the company of others, are easy to talk with, enjoy interaction with others and feel empathy for those with whom they communicate.

It isn't that the *feeler* never listens to advice, it is just that he likes it best when he does his own thing, not someone else's thing. A *feeler* might be classified as one who is driven by emotion and operates spontaneously.

The *thinker* does not give much credence to intuition-driven actions like the *feeler* does. The *thinker* relies on credible sources for the rationale for action. Rationality is the *thinker's* guide. *Thinkers* like it best if others have tried it first, allowing them to review the successes and failures of others' experiences.

The *thinker* is research oriented and well organized—relying heavily on accuracy for all endeavors. She lives a rather structured life and operates with precision on the job, in the home and in other activities of life. The *thinker* is typically a proponent of, and participant in, effective time management. Many a *thinker* keeps a daily journal to record rational thoughts and actions.

The *doer* learns by doing. Once *doers* attempt something, they then make future decisions based upon the results of that attempt. Action is a *doer's* byword, and involvement in things is their theme song. They enjoy involved group discussions but resent such things as seminars dominated by a so-called expert. They often get annoyed by someone who gives them frequent instruction or direction. It is safe to say that *doers* are always busy doing something.

Watchers are the sit-back-and-see learners. They are not in a hurry to make any decisions and do not like for anyone to prod them into making a hurried decision. *Watchers* tend to be introverted—learning best from reading research reports, watching media presentations, attending lectures and carefully reflecting on what is heard and seen. *Watchers* are usually loners who learn best from inward reflection.

It is important to note that an individual's style can change based on his/her situation. We are all a mix of these styles. At times, one might be a *feeler-doer*, while at other times that same person might be a *doer-watcher*, a *doer-thinker* and so forth.

When interacting with another person, it is helpful to understand that person's learning style. Knowing this information helps to avoid a non-productive approach. For example, it would be non-productive to provide abstract theories to the *feeler* and expect the *feeler* to act upon a theory.

One way to help a doer learn is to get her involved in the process or project. Before approaching a *thinker*, prepare a logical, rational theory. Small talk usually does not prove helpful.

Probably the most difficult person to work with is the *watcher*. A *watcher* cannot be pushed into making a decision and you can't expect a lot of interaction from him either. It is best to give *watchers* all the information first, and then allow them time and space to reflect on the information they have received.

The basic difference between the learning styles and the personality styles of individuals is that learning styles teach us things and personality styles are how we apply this knowledge in our actions.

Personality Styles

Personality styles indicate a person's actions to a large degree. They are responses to personality traits. When we know what an individual's personality style is, it can help in our communication with them. It's only logical that if you know how a person may behave or how they like information presented to them, it will help you communicate. This is especially true if you are aware of your own primary personality style.

Each person has one primary personality or social style, but no one is restricted to just one. We are all a combination of two or more of the basic styles. Learning about them will prove helpful to you in formulating your attitude, language choice and emotion for your approach.

If you are aware of your own style, you can alter it somewhat to match the individual with whom you're dealing. This will help the other person trust and respect you more as they will be getting a message from you that mirrors their own way of communicating and behaving.

The four styles we examine here come out of a basic analysis of behavior patterns first observed by Dr. William Moulton Marston's 1928 book, *The Emotions of Normal People.* In this book, Dr. Marston describes four styles or personality patterns that have been universally called DISC.

DISC, as it is used today to analyze social or personality styles, has taken on some more specific characteristics without losing its original concept. that individuals can be carefully observed to determine their primary style.

> **D** = Dominance: The drive to overcome opposing forces of perceived inferior strength to the self.
>
> **I** = Inducement: The attempt to ally forces to ourselves through persuasive means.
>
> **S** = Steadiness: The acquiescence of the self to a perceived allied force.
>
> **C** = Compliance: The subordination of the self to a hostile force of superior strength.

Current Internet searches reveal over 40 variations of the four styles—describing them as colors, animals or even as the points on a compass. Target Training International, Ltd., of Scottsdale, Arizona has hundreds of thousands of individual assessments in their data base. They are a leader in developing processes for assessing, hiring and maintaining work and employee/manager relations based on the DISC profiles.[3]

In TTI's terminology, the styles are commonly reflected as follows:

> **D** = Dominance: This is how a person responds to problems.

I = Influence: This is how a person uses influence or persuasion to have others accept their view.

S = Steadiness: This is how a person responds to what is going on around them in the world.

C = Compliance: This is how a person responds to rules and regulations.

In a study by Dr. David Warburton, he asked people to judge those in different styles with adjectives describing them. While Dr. Warburton did not use DISC specifically, the characteristics of each appear as follows:

D = Dominance: Ambitious, forceful, decisive, direct, independent, and challenging.

I = Influence: Expressive, enthusiastic, friendly, demonstrative, talkative, and stimulating.

S = Steadiness: Methodical, systematic, reliable, steady, relaxed, and modest.

C = Compliance: Analytical, contemplative, conservative, exacting, careful, and deliberate.

When interacting with others, you would do well to consider that person's primary and secondary style. Be aware that each of us is a mixture of styles. There is, however, a dominant style in each of our behavior sets. If you learn to identify and adapt to that individual's style, communication will be more effective.

Intellectual Understanding

If you are to be on the same wavelength as another person and you desire to understand them, you must understand that person intellectually *and* emotionally. Both kinds of understanding are important. You must speak the same language. You cannot play the game of baseball if you each do not agree where second base is located.

Once agreement on the language spoken is achieved, you can be said to have reached *intellectual agreement*. In most corporate interactions, intellectual understanding is pretty much a given.

You probably would not be where you are in your company today if you did not have a good intellectual understanding of what is going on around you. It is rather simple to overcome a lack of intellectual understanding. In most companies, there are facilities, personnel or supported opportunities to learn. Many firms offer tuition assistance to employees who wish to pursue further education in order to help them advance in their job.

Careful study of people, policies, procedures, goals and mission statements of the firm, and product and service manuals can help with intellectual understanding. The escalation of intellectual understanding is a reasonable expectation that an organization should have for its employees. Just because you are promoted to a position, given added responsibilities or moved to a higher floor and given a key to the executive washroom, does not mean that you have arrived.

Why do you think that a graduation ceremony is called a commencement? Are there any *know-it-alls* in your company? Even if it is the CEO, does he or she really know it all?

The semanticist and trainer Irving Lee said decades ago that all declarative sentences should end with et cetera. John Wooden the famous basketball coach would tell his young players, "It is what you learn after you know it all that counts."

Emotional Understanding

Since time immemorial, the corporate philosophy on intelligence has been dominated by an emphasis on intellectual intelligence. The IQ factor has played a part in the hiring, promotion, retention and general acceptance of personnel. The leading accounting firms in the United States won't even consider an applicant whose grade point average falls below a certain level—usually an A-.

Most graduate programs at major universities require at least a B+ average in the student's undergraduate career.

Law schools and medical schools make their first cuts of applicants from those with the lowest grades.

We're not suggesting that achieving success in your academic classes is not important. It should not be the sole determinant of potential success in one's chosen field.

In many progressive and successful corporations today, your emotional quotient or EQ, as it is commonly called, has become more than just a buzzword. It's been incorporated into the training programs of leadership and coaching.

It is stressed by most proponents of Emotional Intelligence that EQ is more important as a harbinger of success than is IQ, the old standard by which we used to measure people. Dr. Daniel Goleman of Harvard, who is widely recognized as the foremost researcher of Emotional Intelligence, has proven that, as a determiner of success, IQ is only 10% while EQ is 90%.[4]

We've already discussed the possibility that intellectual intelligence can be increased. It can be achieved by anyone with the desire, commitment and fortitude to make it happen.

Could it be possible that emotional intelligence can also be learned? We believe that it can, and that it can prove beneficial to the organization and, therefore, should be incorporated into the growth program of any firm.

What is emotional intelligence? It is that part of an individual's nature that allows her to understand, relate to, control and manage her emotions.

It also allows him to recognize emotional responses and what they imply in others. This allows them to function in working with others to help encourage excellence.

When you are aware of your emotions, when you take control of them, manage them, are aware of the intricacies of social connections and are able to manage relationships on the job, as well as in other key areas of your life, you can be said to be emotionally intelligent.

The following are the four areas that define emotional intelligence: self-awareness, self-management, social awareness, and relationship management.

Self-Awareness

The artist painting a pastoral scene paints for a little while, and then steps back away from his work to view it from a distance. He paints some more and steps back once again.

Her reason for stepping back is not to pat herself on the back for the upcoming masterpiece; it is to look objectively at the painting in order to get a perspective on the work in progress.

This is what we must do if we are to become aware of our emotions. If we are not aware of our emotions, we cannot do much about managing them.

There is a reason why self-awareness is the first step in gaining emotional intelligence. If we are going to make positive adjustments in our thinking and behavior, it is imperative that we look with an unbiased eye at how we feel and react to situations from an emotional perspective.

Think back in your life to a particularly embarrassing

moment. How did you feel? Were you humiliated? Did others mock you? What actions did you take to regain the respect of those who shared in your moment of shame?

Think of an embarrassing experience you have had at work. Can you relive the pain of the moment? Have you ever made the same mistake again? How did you handle the situation? How did you feel? Have you learned to view the emotions that you experienced at that time with a judgmental eye?

Reliving those uncomfortable moments in your life is necessary in your search for emotional self-awareness. If you get angry, hurt, mortified, disgusted or testy when things do not go your way, you need to be aware of it. It can be painful to do a self-examination. Living in ignorance regarding where those emotions stem from is so much more comfortable. And yet, if you can get past the pain of reliving those moments and identifying the source of the emotions, you are well on your way to releasing those uncomfortable memories as merely a part of the past, and you're closer to managing your emotions effectively.

Accept the fact that you are human. Emotions are a part of the human experience. In most instances, the emotions serve us well. We feel love, satisfaction, beauty, honor, joy and happiness because we are emotional beings. Become aware of all of your emotional buttons. When you can do this, you have taken the first step toward the goal of managing them.

Self-Management

Do animals have emotions? I suspect so. I cannot imagine two big-horned rams butting heads without some emotion being present. It is one thing for a sheep to act this way to demonstrate his dominance over the ewes in his flock, but it is quite another for the department head to butt heads with the CEO, a fellow manager or a subordinate, in order to get his way.

It is natural that we get upset when we perceive a threat against our credibility, our position or our reputation. If we are managing our emotions, we aren't forced to decide between of *fight* or *flight*.

We, unlike bighorn sheep, have many alternatives. The first is perhaps our Maker's greatest gift to mankind: free will. We are free to choose our own way. We are free to choose to manage our emotions rather than to let them manage us.

When we are able to sit back and become an observer of our emotions—some of which might even make us laugh, if we are big enough to laugh at ourselves—we will be in charge. We can then use our emotions for action instead of reaction.

If things do not seem to be going too well for you on the job, in your home or in other social settings, maybe it is time for you to be aware of how you are managing your emotions. Remember this, you are the captain of your own ship, and you set the sail according to the direction you choose to go. Perhaps the following poem can describe this process.

The Set of the Sails

Consider this fact in the cosmos wide
That a forest great in one seed resides.
Don't be amazed, it's no mystery,
That creation itself resides in thee.

Take just one step, or wave your hand,
The world will change, right where you stand.
The power you hold is great indeed,
To create a flower, or enhance a weed.

Each word you utter is a sacred bond,
That manipulates matter, it's a magic wand.
Yours to make joyous, or bring forth pain,
By what you say in your daily reign.

Take care, beloved, now and ever more,
Traveling onward to your chosen shore.
If your thoughts are anxious, this truth prevails,
It's not the wind that guides you, it's the set of your sails.

— Jim Mayfield —

Social-Awareness

When we consider a person to possess social awareness, we see them as having the ability to build meaningful relationships with people of all kinds. Socially aware individuals view themselves in positive ways, possess a healthy self-image, have a solid work ethic and treat others as they wish to be treated, with kindness, understanding and empathy.

Those who are socially aware express a genuine care for other people, supporting them in their efforts to succeed, while keeping their ego in check. They are ever ready to assist and work with others for the common good and for the good of the corporation.

They operate on the basis of fairness in their dealings with others. They have the ability to readily engender the support of others in resolving conflicts. A person that possesses social awareness recognizes that communication is a process where A says something to B, and B responds to A.

They are aware that true two-way communication produces results that are usually observable and can often be measured.

A meaningful definition of verbal communication, as stated in the beginning of this book, is "Who says what to whom with what effect." The person who is socially aware understands that people are different in many ways. Some of these are listed below.

Learning styles	Home life
Background	Lifestyle
Economic condition	Aspirations
Experience	Emotional maturity
Personality	Ethical perspective
Dreams	Values
Personality Styles	Visions
Interests	Hopes
Education	Communication skills

The socially aware person accepts these differences, adjusts her behavior with others, not in order to change others, but to relate more effectively with them. She looks beyond the flaws of others into their potential. She knows people. She likes people. And she finds satisfaction in helping them achieve their goals.

If the characteristics of the socially aware person are not in your arsenal of social weapons, perhaps you could work on those you believe would help you in your relationship with others. There are many books and classes now available on improving your emotional intelligence.

Relationship Management

As we noted before, in order to manage your emotions, you must be aware of their existence and the power they have over your behavior. Before you can manage relationships with others you must possess social awareness. You can't manage anything effectively without understanding the components of what you hope to manage.

Can you imagine Tiger Woods reaching into his golf bag,

pulling out a sand wedge and saying, "I wonder what this is for." How about a pilot of a giant 747 saying to his copilot, "Good grief, there must be 200 dials, levers and switches here. I think I'll flip this switch and see what happens." And then the surgeon exclaiming, "I wish now that I hadn't cheated my way through anatomy class. Which one of these things in here is the bladder and which is the liver?" Do you get the idea? We can't manage something we know nothing about.

Perhaps the greatest boon to relationship management would be for the emotionally intelligent person to possess empathetic ability. This ability to "walk in someone else's moccasins" is invaluable in managing relationships.

To understand another's values, beliefs, perceptions, motives and actions provides a door of opportunity for communicating effectively. When you are able to "mentally enter into the feeling or spirit of a person", you will possess an outstanding tool kit with which to enhance your relationship with them.

To express empathy toward another person is to listen to them and relate to them with your total being while you're communicating. To do this takes considerable time, effort and commitment, but the payoff can be tremendous.

Those who have made the commitment to empathize with others report amazing changes in their relationships. Family members, husbands and wives, parents and children, in-laws, neighbors, friends, co-workers, subordinates and superiors, all have benefited. Rifts have been repaired, slights have been forgiven and hostilities and hatreds have been replaced by peace and love. The use of empathy in managing relationships is a powerful communication tool.

One method of practicing empathy is to intellectually and emotionally reverse your role with another person. Recall some rather significant disagreement you have had with someone that you know quite well. Perhaps this might be someone in your family, or someone at work.

Think of a situation that caused you considerable discomfort and, perhaps, has not been fully resolved as yet. It does not matter who was at fault in the matter. Practice empathy to increase your understanding of another person, and review what transpired.

Consider another approach that might be taken to resolve the situation. Close your eyes, take a deep breath, reserve judgment, take your ego out of the equation and enter into the spirit of the other person.

Method acting asks the aspiring actor to become something as unsuspecting as a tree. Now that the actor has mentally become a tree, the actor examines his purpose on earth: to bear fruit. He feels his roots being nourished by the fertile loam. He senses the sunlight shining on his verdant leaves. He is awesomely aware of his branches as they reach outward and upward as if in thankful prayer. The aroma of the blossoms pleases him as they foretell the fruit that will soon burden his branches. He is saddened by the sound of the woodsman's axe close by. He knows he is losing a friend. He is somewhat fearful that the woodsman might consider him next. As a tree, knowing the tree from the inside out, he is now in a position to communicate effectively with the tree.

In a similar exercise, try to relive an uncomfortable situation by placing yourself in the innermost feelings and workings of the other person. Now that you are the *other* person, ask yourself some questions.

- Why did I say that?

- Why did I do that?

- Why did I take offense at what you said?

- Why did I react so strongly to what you said?

- What was there in my value system, belief inventory or moral position that caused me to go to war with you?

- What did I want to happen?

- Why didn't it happen the way I wanted it to?

- What would I do if you came to me and we tried it again?

- Would I react the same way?

If you were honest projecting yourself into the mind of the other person, you probably have a better understanding of what went wrong in the experience. Empathy works! It can prove useful as you commit to managing your relationships more effectively.

Emotional understanding can be yours by practicing *emotional intelligence.* In review, the four steps necessary are *self-awareness,* looking objectively at your emotions; *self-management,* taking charge of your emotions and controlling them in your dealings with other people and situations; *social-awareness,* learning all you can about people and what makes them tick; and *relationship-management,* learning and using the how, when, why, where and to whom you should apply empathy when dealing with others.

CHAPTER 5:

EMPOWERING

> To exist is to snuggle comfortably in the swaddling clothes of the status quo. To truly live is to confront your possibilities.
> *Joe Batten - Expectations and Possibilities*

T he American College Dictionary defines *empower* as "to make able; give power, means or ability to; make competent; authorize; to make possible or easy." We must also take a look at the opposite of empower: *disable*. Disable is defined as "to make unable; weaken or destroy the capability of; cripple; incapacitate."

Why begin with definitions? When talking about *empowering*, we must know what it is we are doing to empower someone or what we might be doing to disable someone.

Abraham Lincoln attended church one Sunday in Washington and heard a well-known minister speak. When asked what he thought of the sermon, President Lincoln replied, "Since you've asked, I must confess I didn't think much of it." When asked why, Lincoln replied, "Because {the minister} didn't ask us to do anything great."

The following poem by an unknown author certainly strikes a chord when considering what life offers. For an enabler, whether personally or professionally, the mundane should only be a stepping stone to greatness.

I bargained with life for a penny
And life would pay no more.
However I begged at evening,
When I counted my scanty store.
For life is a just employer
It pays you what you ask,
But once you set the wages,
Then you must bear the task.
I worked for a menial's hire,
Only to find, dismayed,
That anything I had asked of life,
Life would have gladly paid.— Anonymous

Discovering peoples' desires and their wildest expectations is essential before you can help them achieve what their minds have conceived. Discovering those wild expectations is the first step in communicating to them that they are valued, and it's the first step toward helping them realize their dreams.

Seemingly wild expectations have yielded a standard of living that we enjoy today. Who could have imagined that man could fly? Orville and Wilbur Wright imagined it, pursued it and, with the help of others, realized it!

Who could have supposed that the debilitating disease of polio (poliomyelitis) could be literally wiped out in the United States by a vaccine? Dr. Jonas Salk imagined it, pursued it, and with the help of others, did it!

Who could have conceived of someone walking on the moon? President John F. Kennedy imagined it. And although he did not live long enough to see the dream realized, his words and actions empowered others to see the dream come true!

Who could have imagined that voices could be transmitted through wires? Alexander Graham Bell did!

And the list of "who could imagine" is really endless. Who could have dreamed of such things as computers, super-sonic airplanes or cat scans that can see deeply into the workings of the human body? Who could have imagined the pacemaker, an electronic metronome that has saved so many lives?

In spite of all the marvels of our contemporary world, we can have so much more than what we have. Perhaps we could discover a cure for one of the many diseases that plague our world today. Perhaps we could put an end to world hunger, except for the want of someone who will dream it, pursue it and achieve it! But don't misunderstand; setting high expectations does not mean you have to be unhappy with what you have.

It is unfortunate that so many people are unhappy with what they now possess. Much unhappiness stems from feelings brought on by a perceived lack in life. In fact, focusing on one's lack is more closely linked to weak and mundane expectations, often practiced out of habit. And although some habits are useful and necessary—such as the habit of dressing or personal hygiene—other habits can actually stifle creativity. Doing something that has always been done a certain way is often counter-productive. "If you always do what you've always done, you'll always have what you've already got."

Being content with one's circumstances and still being able to set and pursue high expectations is certainly a delicate balance. This is why some people achieve their highest dreams while others don't even have any.

What then can be done to inspire others to see beyond their self-imposed boundaries? Empowering. Yes, empowering another person to break out of tradition and empowering them to discover the best in themselves is a high calling. Robert Frost, a premier American poet put it this way, "Something we were withholding made us weak until we found it was ourselves."

Another contributing factor to some people settling for the mediocre in life, is a low self-image. Some people have come to see themselves as *less than able*. John Kehoe, in his book *Mind Power*[5] lists three mindsets that can help build a positive self-image. These are useful as stepping stones to winning someone's trust and confidence and useful for empowering someone to dream big dreams.

First, you are *unique*. No one else has your thoughts, your ideas or your exact way of doing things. You are not ordinary, you are extraordinary. Second, *you can do anything*. You can travel anywhere, learn any language, start any business, learn to play any musical instrument, join any group, learn any craft, develop any trade, change careers, begin and finish any project and, very importantly, you can think any thoughts. And third, *you have unlimited power*. Every day of your life you wake up with unlimited power at your disposal. You can create, build and strengthen any area of your life. Where you are, creation is!

Sharing these mindsets with others is one way of *empowering*. It has been said that success helps many people, but failure helps no one. Father James Keller (1900-1977) Founder, The Christophers said, "A candle loses nothing by lighting another candle."

Empowering others can be done by suggesting, not ordering; leading, not driving; freeing, not enslaving; clearing, not crowding; inviting, not confronting; and supporting dreams, not breaking them.

PUTTING IT INTO PRACTICE

I would like to offer a personal example of *empowering* in action. My son Ryan was four years old and attending pre-school. One particular day, I stopped to pick him up, but he was nowhere to be found inside the building.

I went outside and heard his voice but could not immediately locate him. He was singing. I followed the sound of his voice, and looked up to see him swinging from the limbs of a tree at least 20 feet off of the ground. It would be an understatement to say that I was frightened by the sight of my young son hanging like a monkey from a tree limb, singing at the top of his lungs, apparently unafraid. I was horrified.

The playground teacher saw my reaction, and stopped me before I could yell at Ryan to come down and before I could lecture him on the potential dangers of such a stunt. That day, the teacher taught me a lesson I shall never forget. It is one that I have tried to put into practice whenever dealing with my wonderful son who is now a young adult and my hero. The teacher said to me, "You can heal a broken arm, but you can never heal a broken spirit. Whatever restraints you place on your son now will likely be with him for the rest of his life."

The teacher taught me that my son has to have the opportunity to fail. The same is true for everyone. If people are not ever given the opportunity to try, how do they know what they can accomplish? I am sorry to admit that more than once I have misjudged a person's potential. I have watched in horror as some of those people lived *down* to my expectations. I believe the greatest sign of a true leader is being able to see others' potential and then *empowering* them to accomplish their best.

There is nothing more honorable, more productive, or more thrilling than to see the best in people. This empowers them to fulfill their maximum potential by providing motivation, resources and the opportunity for them to be their best.

Why has IBM been so successful in an industry full of companies eager to usurp this giant's power? Thomas Watson, Jr., the past CEO of IBM, speaks to this issue. In his book, *Business and Its Beliefs* [6], he states, "I want to begin with what I think is the most important (belief), our respect for the individual. This is a simple concept, but in IBM it occupies a major portion of management time. We devote more effort to it than to anything else."

What is really taking place at IBM, and in every other successful enterprise from Mrs. Young's third grade class at Entz Elementary School in Mesa, Arizona to John McArthur's Grace Community Church in Sun Valley, California, is respecting, honoring and empowering people to become all that they wish to be and all that they are capable of becoming.

Easing the path that leads someone toward an accomplishment, whether large or small, is one way of *empowering*. Sometimes it is only a matter of authorizing someone to carry out an activity. It is that simple. *Empowering* is a great adventure! And *empowering* others not only supports and enhances the individual being *empowered*, but a wonderful by-product is that it also "ennobles" us.

The opposite is also true. When we fail to authorize someone's action, such as forbidding a child to climb a tree, we can be said to be *disabling*. Providing a *hold-back* is also disabling. What is a hold-back? Perhaps the following story will explain it.

In the early 1990's, I was doing some training for the United States Navy in Corpus Christie, Texas. After completing the training, I became aware of a program that the Navy had instituted. It was an opportunity to visit an aircraft carrier. I completed the necessary paper work and was invited to fly from Beeville, Texas aboard a C –1, COD (transport plane) and land on the aircraft carrier, USS Lexington. Needless to say, it was one of those experiences that I shall never forget.

After an abrupt landing on the USS Lexington, the six of us in the party were invited to meet the captain of the carrier and observe the operations on the giant ship. As planes landed and took off from the carrier's deck, we observed that from time to time the entire deck crew locked arms and walked the entire length of the carrier. We were told they were looking for any debris that might cause problems for take-offs and landings. A piece of that debris is something called a *hold-back*. It is a small barbell-shaped piece of metal, about 8-to-10 inches long. Each plane is equipped with a bracket that attaches to one end of the hold-back, while the other end is connected to the catapult. The hold-back is milled so when the pressure from the steam-driven catapult builds to the right pressure, the hold-back breaks. The catapult is then released, and the plane is sent streaking off the ship.

I keep a hold-back on my desk as a souvenir from my adventure. I also keep it to remind me that there are things in my life that try to prevent me from flying high. During my quiet moments of meditation, I try to identify the hold-backs in my life, and consider ways to build up enough steam to break them loose.

When interacting with others, try to identify possible hold-backs in them. And then, consider what would provide steam for their catapult to help them launch, thereby *empowering* them.

Sometimes it is a skill issue. Often it is a matter of attitude that prevents someone from taking off. Sometimes it is a personal problem that, if talked out with someone who cares, can be resolved, or at least, made tolerable. Sometimes it is merely a need to have someone value them in order for them to value themselves. And sometimes it is a need for someone to let them know what is expected of them, assuring them that they can accomplish what is expected, and then holding them accountable.

Expectations play an important role in a person's life. And it is important for us to help increase others' expectations by seeing their unrealized potential, identifying any self-imposed limitations and empowering them to see the possibilities.

After all, expectations are what drive us all. We would not get very far if we did not have expectations to drive us forward. Imagine getting into your car to go to work without expecting it to start. Imagine driving on the freeway without expecting the other drivers to obey the rules of the highway. Imagine taking medicine without expecting it to alleviate the problem.

One of life's great truths is, "A person tends to become precisely what he or she expects to become." Does that shock you? It shouldn't. Think of your own life. Think back to the expectations you set for yourself. There were some for school, sports, friendships, family, marriage and career.

What good things ever happened to you without first expecting them to happen? Luck may sometimes play a part in our lives, but most things that happen to us are guided by our expectations.

Setting expectations for yourself is a powerful way to make things happen in your life. You can also set expectations for others. That is a good way to empower someone. Where did our early expectations come from? Where did your early expectations in your professional life come from? Believe me, they didn't fall out of an empty sky, and they weren't delivered to you by carrier pigeon. Someone else was responsible for many of your early expectations.

Your life's early expectations came from many sources such as your parents, teachers, pastors, friends, family, co-workers, bosses and employees. If any of these people valued you, they told you so, maybe not in so many words, but through their actions and affirmations and they communicated to you that you are valued.

Good expectations come from people who care about other people. Sometimes those who help you set expectations do not even realize that is what they are doing. They simply see potential in you and communicate the potential they have observed. This causes you to see what they see, and, consequently, you raise your level of expectation to align with *their* vision of you. And yet, when you really get down to it, expectations come from your own beliefs and your own thinking about what you want for your life.

Our higher expectations, those that really make a difference in our lives, find their basis in the successes we enjoy. Success breeds success.

When we achieve an accomplishment that fulfills an expectation, we tend to raise our sights and set higher expectations. Conversely, when we fail to achieve a goal, it tends to lower our ability to heighten our expectations. We need to develop the attitude that failing does not make us a failure.

Many of us have been told by those we love that we are dumb, fat, ugly, clumsy, etc. We internalize those things and set our expectations accordingly. I am sure you have heard a mother yell at her child, "You are so stupid." How many times does a child need to hear that before he or she internalizes it and sets her expectations accordingly?

As adults, we have failures; we are told that we "can't." All of those things take a toll on how we perceive ourselves and how we set our expectations. We have to find a way to perform above the limits set on us by others and ourselves. It is within our power to change. We can go to the edge of our expectations and then step across the line. To do so, we must deliberately *raise* expectations, sometimes beyond what we believe we can achieve.

Robert Browning, the English Victorian poet wrote, "Our reach should exceed our grasp, or what's a heaven for?" If your horse is going to jump over a three-foot fence, how high must he jump? It had better be more than three feet! In order to build muscles, create flexibility or utilize aerobic conditioning, stretching is necessary. A weight trainer's motto is, "No pain, no gain." Expectations are much the same.

Our highest gain comes with the minor effort of seeing ourselves as somewhat better than we are and working to achieve this new vision. The same is true when empowering others; they need to be encouraged to reach beyond their grasp.

During creative problem solving, one of the holdbacks of thinking creatively is called a *mind-binder*. Mind-binders are negative statements that communicate that something cannot be done. Here are some examples:

- I'm too old to learn a new trade.

- I tried that once and failed.

- Uncle Jack tried to make that work on his car and it didn't, so I'm certainly not going to make that mistake too.

- Sure I've got some ideas on how to improve production, but I'm not going to show them to the boss, because he'll just put me down again.

- I'm not going to rock the boat because the last time I did, I nearly drowned.

Take any of these mind-binders, and see if you can construct a positive expectation from it. It's impossible, isn't it?

The American humorist Will Rogers was speaking to some would-be salespeople. He said, "If you're traveling down the highway, and you don't know where you're going, pull off the road 'cause you've already arrived at your destination." Setting expectations for what we want to accomplish helps us know where we want to go.

There is a direct correlation between the quality of planning and the effectiveness of the execution. Before you left home this morning, what specific expectations did you set for yourself? What things did you plan that you wanted to happen? Has someone asked you today, "What do you want to happen at work today?" Can you imagine someone suggesting to you that you might consider what you expect to accomplish at work, instead of going to work and having the day attack you with a bunch of little surprises?

For example, let's say you have a meeting scheduled with the head of maintenance to tell him that he has to cut one member of his crew. Ouch! He is really going to be ticked off. Perhaps if you first let him tell you how his crew functions and where he sees its strengths and weaknesses, you might discover that he would be more amenable to the necessary change.

Maybe if you ask the right questions, listen carefully to his responses, show him you understand his position and explain the problem from the company's point of view, he might be more willing to cooperate with you.

When you share high expectations you have for someone else, you are, in fact, honoring that person by letting him or her know you trust them and believe they can accomplish what you suggest. Give others something to reach for, and more than likely, they will stretch to reach it.

A junior high school teacher in the Midwest also tested the idea that expectations can empower students to do better. Her assignment in the school included one class for gifted students (students with a high IQ) and three other classes randomly assigned from student enrollment. She selected one of the average classes to use in her experiment.

On the first day of class, she gave the following remarks, "Welcome students. I'm really glad all of you have been assigned to my special class. You don't know how much pleasure it gives me to be challenged by super learners like you. I'm honored to work with you and to learn from you. When the principal assigned you to this class, he and I discussed how I was going to approach such a gifted group of young people. I told him that I was going to provide materials that would challenge you, and I would try to provide guidance that would let you be yourself and that I would encourage you to work at your highest level possible. We are proud to have you attending this school, and we know you are going to succeed this semester like you have never before succeeded. I'm laying down the challenge. Are you super students willing to pick it up?"

The results of her class experiment were amazing! The students in that particular class scored 22% higher on their achievement tests in her subject—language arts—than did the other two average classes she taught. The most outstanding result was that this class of average IQ students scored 6% higher than her *gifted* (high IQ) class.

The point cannot be missed here. If you provide challenges for others and communicate your expectations that are somewhat higher than they believe they can fulfill, they will almost always rise to the occasion. This is another way of empowering someone to achieve all that they can be!

Similar to a horse needing to jump higher than three feet

in order to clear a three-foot fence, teachers often design lesson plans a grade higher than the grade in which the children are currently enrolled. In this way, the students can be guided to stretch their thinking and learning expectations higher than they think they can be. Indeed, a person's reach should always exceed their grasp.

Another great example of high expectations is world-class diver Laura Wilkinson. While she was preparing for her 10-meter platform dive in the 2000 Summer Olympics, she broke 3 toes. Not able to get into the water, Laura sat on the side of the pool for hours and visualized every move, every thought and every sensation. She knew that she had just one chance. As the world looked on with amazement, she performed her medal dive flawlessly and took home the gold medal.

One of the statements John F. Kennedy is remembered for comes from his inaugural address. "Ask not what your country can do for you. Ask what you can do for your country." That directive said a lot about pride of country, patriotism and responsibility. It caused lots of people to reassess what this great country had given to them, the freedoms, opportunities, and challenges. Perhaps we can adapt his wonderful challenge to our search for ways of empowering others. "Ask not what someone can do for you, but ask what you can do for that person."

Have you ever been guilty of being a *disabler* rather than an *empowerer?* Have you ever doused someone else's flame? Have you ever hindered someone else's hunch? Have you ever been a stifled someone else's striving? If you have, perhaps it is time to change.

Ask good, open-ended questions to discover a person's expectations. Then, set about helping them fulfill and expand those expectations to encompass greater challenges.

Look deeply into the potential of an individual so you can help them to reach their goal. Empower them, authorize them and make it possible.

Do not let someone else's limitations move in on them. Help them to constantly excel toward their highest possibilities. Do not promise anyone the world. Instead, help them win it by empowering them. There is not a more noble calling. Make it happen!

CHAPTER 6

SERVING

The Servant King

They called on me to lead them, I said "Where shall we go?"
They wept aloud, and cried all night. Then said "We do not know."
The wind is blowing eastward. The forest is in the west.
The bluebird's flying southward, having left his northern nest.
The mountains are above us. The plains stretch far and wide.
"I know not where to lead you. This truth I must confide."
"We only know we need you. We cannot tell you why.
Unless you heed our calling, we will surely die."
They gave me cloak and mantle, and a robe with purple hue,
A scepter, crown, and silver, to which a king is due.
I watched my people labor, from dawn to darkest night.
I felt their pain and hunger, and saw their fearsome plight.
I watched them from the throne room, their planting on the moor.
I even waved my royal hand, but never left my door.
I gloried in my riches, and ate my steak and pie.
I even wept to show I cared, when one of them did die.
One night in royal chambers, shone forth a brilliant light.
A voice from out of nowhere, "What you do, it is not right".
You can hardly know their anguish when you view them from afar.
To be their king, know this my liege, you must be where they are.
I doffed my royal raiment. I laid my crown aside.
I journeyed to the valley, there determined to abide.
Just being there beside them with their heartbeat in my ears,
I nursed my wounded brothers, and wiped away their tears.
I borrowed pick and shovel, and sowed the precious grain.
I kissed the soil on my hands, and prayed for gentle rain.
The people gathered round me, as we heard the angels sing.
Then once again the voice I heard, "You are the servant-king."

—Jim Mayfield —

The great humanitarian Dr. Albert Schweitzer said on one occasion, "I don't know what your destiny will be, but one thing I do know. The only ones among you who will be really happy are those who will have sought and found how to serve." And to restate views on one's purpose, "Man's purpose on earth is to serve mankind."

The definition of a leader is "a guiding or directing head." With this definition in mind, indeed, we are all leaders of one kind or another. In this respect, we must not be hindered by the fact that not everyone is formally designated as a leader. And so, whether formally or informally, as leaders, it is our privilege and responsibility to serve those we lead.

If you are a **parent,** you are a leader. If you are a **salesperson,** you are a leader. If you are a **customer service representative,** you are a leader. If you are a **CEO, vice president manager,** or **supervisor,** you are a leader.

Anytime you act to get something done through others, you are a leader. And the one thing that successful leaders do to get the greatest results in any situation is to serve those they lead.

People obey a master if they are slaves, regardless of the service provided to them by the master. People in this generation might do what they are told, but they very likely will not do anything extra. In fact, most people do very little if their leader tells them what to do and provides no service to them. Gone are the days of "do it now, and do it my way, or else!" No matter whom you are leading, or in what situation you are leading them, you need to be aware of what is in it for *them*, rather than what is in it for *you*. One of the most important points we can remember as managers, is that "we can buy a person's hands, but not their heart." That is to say, if you pay a person well, they will perform the task they were hired to perform. But, if you expect them to engage their heart when they show up for work, you have to earn their trust and respect through serving them.

Leadership is the art and science of accomplishing tasks through people. This is done by seeing the best in others, honoring and valuing them and creating an environment where they can be successful.

The ultimate way to accomplish tasks is to identify what motivates those you are leading, find out their motivational needs, meet those needs and help them be successful. It is not always easy to discover those motivational needs. Sometimes it might be necessary to look beyond your own biases.

You might not even *like* the person you are leading. Your past experiences with that person may have been a disaster. You might not trust that person. Maybe they have given you reasons not to trust them; perhaps even having betrayed you in the past. You might believe that they are incompetent, unworthy or lazy.

That is the bad news in having to work with them. The good news is that you do not have to like them in order to lead them. You do not have to trust them. What you do have to do is go outside of your own feelings, determine their needs and go about the business of meeting those needs.

Of course, this is *not* easy to do. It takes a lot of inner confidence to do it. You have to swallow ego, pride, hate, mistrust and any other negative feeling or emotion that arises when you think about working with that person. You might not be able to keep from feeling as you do, but you can determine how you act on those feelings. A good leader, parent, coach, boss or teacher does not let negative feelings interfere with the task at hand.

For example, you might be infuriated with your son for mouthing off at you. You might have exhausted the punishments you can assign to him such as grounding him for a week, no television for a month, or no Internet access for a month. And yet, he still hasn't finished his homework. Whether you presently feel amiable toward him or not, it is your job to get him to do it. He might do the work if you order him to do it, but it is more likely that he will learn something from the homework if he has a good attitude while he's doing it.

Leader power might get someone to do the job at the lowest level of production, but servant power—that is, discovering unmet needs associated with the task—might work better to get someone to function at a higher level. There are two types of power that leaders have: personal power and positional power.

Positional power may get the task done, but personal power will get it done with the right attitude. We have all worked with people who, while they may have had the title of manager, had no personal power. You may have also worked for someone who created an environment that met your needs in such a way that you performed above and beyond what was expected of you. That leader had personal power.

One way to create that personal power is to be genuinely interested in people. Care about their problems. Ask in a non-threatening, non-authoritarian way, what problems they might have with a task, and they might tell you. You might discover an unmet need. Notice that the phrase is unmet *needs*, not unmet *wants*.

Needs and wants are not the same. Let's look at another parenting example. A teenager might *want* to stay out until 11:30 p.m., but she *needs* to get adequate sleep. She might *want* to spend three hours talking on her cell phone to friends, but she *needs* to get her homework done. She might *want* to eat nothing but fast food, but she *needs* to have a well-balanced diet.

It is much the same way in the corporate world. An employee might _want_ a raise, but he _needs_ to have the trust and support of his supervisors. She might _want_ to have everything done her way, but she _needs_ to work with her team, sharing ideas and making decisions that will benefit the company and its employees. He might _want_ to transfer to another department, but he _needs_ to have someone coach him on his present job, talk to him about the value of his actions and help him to reach potential within the firm.

The servant leader considers the wants, but is concerned with the _needs_ of his followers. If it is the _needs_ the leader is looking for, with the intention of meeting them, it will be easier for the leader to overlook associated feelings and emotions and to focus on taking positive and productive actions to meet those needs.

Let's take a look at the kinds of needs that human beings have. Abraham Maslow wrote what is now called Maslow's _Hierarchy of Needs_. In it, he claims that human needs exist at various progressive levels. And until the lower levels are met, it is pretty much a waste of time to use the higher level needs as motivators for action.

- **Level One—Bodily needs.** These are what we need to stay alive. They include food, water, clothing and shelter from the elements.

- **Level Two—Safety and security needs.** This is the feel-safe level. These needs can include locks on our doors, insurance, police protection, protective shoes and so forth.

- **Level Three—Love and belongingness needs.** These needs inspire us to get married and have a family, join a club, join a bowling league, go out for lunch with our colleagues, talk to our neighbor over the backyard fence and so forth.

- **Level Four—Ego and self-esteem needs.** We work hard to accept ourselves. We look at the way other people see us. These needs inspire us to care about the way we dress, to get haircuts and to buy certain items. Most of the time, people will do just about anything to make themselves feel better.

- **Level Five—Self-actualization needs.** This one is more difficult to define. Even Maslow refused to explain what he meant by self-actualization. Most students of Maslow assume that this represents the high point of a person's life. Self actualization is when all the other needs have been met; when people are well-fed, safe, love, and satisfied with self, they are free to be creative and fulfilled. This is where you can realize your full potential."

In a later discussion, Maslow hinted that this might be equivalent to happiness. And he is noted for saying, "What a man [speaking generically] can be, he must be." Some of his serious students have interpreted this to mean that if someone wishes to be happy, she has to fulfill her potential.

What do human *needs*, as described in Maslow's *Hierarchy of Needs*, have to do with getting things done through people? Plenty!

Needs are basic to all humanity. If a person has a problem, we can be relatively certain that it falls within one of the hierarchy levels. This means that if we skillfully ask the right questions, we can probably uncover a person's needs. These needs could include not being accepted by their peers at work, not being valued and appreciated at home or elsewhere, constantly being disabled by a significant figure in their childhood, not feeling safe at home through spousal or parental abuse, not receiving praise for what they do well, no one caring enough to ask what they like or dislike, not eating or sleeping well, etc.

The point is, when we realize that every person's needs are somehow related to the hierarchy of needs, we can use this knowledge to discover the needs and serve that person. As we know, oftentimes we must put our own *wants* aside if we are to meet the *needs* of someone else. For example, a mother might scrubs floors and take in washing to send her child to college.

Several years ago in Flagstaff, Arizona, I met a wonderful Native American girl. Her mother was a master rug weaver. The rugs that Maria brought for us to see were absolutely beautiful! She explained that two of them had taken eight months to complete! Her mother, a single parent with five children, had put four children through college and graduate school with her rug weaving skills. All four of Maria's siblings had earned doctorates. Two were physicians, one an attorney and one a college professor. The mother did all of this with the money she earned weaving rugs.

Do you suppose that the mother, who was meeting her children's needs, might have, at some juncture or the other, *wanted* to do something else? Do you think she might have been exhausted some afternoon and *wanted* to take a nap? Do you suppose she might have *wanted* to go shopping to buy something for her own pleasure? Well, she didn't. Not ever. She gave her all—body, mind, spirit and energy—to fill the *needs* she saw in her children. She served them, and hopefully fulfilled her own needs while doing so.

How could she have convinced five children to undertake such a momentous thing as getting an education in a culture that was foreign to their own? She must have earned their respect and trust for them to go that far. This mother was a leader in every sense of the word. And of course, there are many more examples of meeting other's *needs* while putting aside one's own *wants*, such as Mother Teresa and the gift she gave of herself to the poor in India.

The effective leader is one who discovers and meets the *needs* of others in order to achieve some purpose that provides benefit. He does this while ignoring dislikes, grudges, selfishness and ego, and he opens up communication that centers on the problem or issue at hand.

The effective leader is one who serves others, who, for the time being, keeps her own *wants* under wraps so the job can get done. The effective leader is a servant to her followers, and by serving others, she wins the game of leadership.

CHAPTER 7

LEADERSHIP WITH V.A.L.U.E.S.

> True leaders bring people along, no matter what their qualities are, and raise them to a higher standard. *J. Richard Munro*

W e can be definitive in our analysis of leadership. A leader is an agent of change. An effective leader, by any definition, is one who takes others from Point A to Point B with positive strides that result in positive gains.

Management is something else. This is not to say that a manager cannot be an effective leader. Hopefully, the manager can manage and lead! The manager *might* be a hands-on person, but the leader *always* is. The manager is assigned to his or her role, and sometimes basks in it. The leader may also have been assigned to a role, but she does not sit back and watch. She jumps in and joins others in reaching the goal, accomplishing the project. A leader—whether formally appointed as a manager or informally leading coworkers on the task at hand—is an enlightened employee with a philosophy of success that is evident to everyone around him.

A leader is a motivator, a communicator, a model of thought and behavior, a *valuer*, a quality controller, a creative force, a team builder, a visionary, an empowerer, a risk-taker, a coach and a counselor. A leader must also be able to see what is, what can be, and what should be. She is able to view situations from all directions, east, west, north and south.

Perhaps it is a given that leaders need followers. It is a simple statement, but one that some leaders might consider reflecting on—whether in business, education, religion, politics or family life structure. An individual cannot be a leader without at least one follower. When mulling this over, a potential leader hopefully recognizes the awesome responsibility he has to reach out and encourage those followers, meeting their needs and healing whatever discord that exists in and around them.

No one can say it better than Tom Peters and Robert Waterman in their exciting book *In Search of Excellence*[7], a compilation of outstanding organizations and why they are so successful. "Treat people as adults. Treat them as partners, treat them with dignity, and treat them with respect...If you want productivity and the financial reward that goes with it, you must treat your workers as your most important asset."

Leaders, like all employees in the firm, must be held accountable for their actions and the results of those actions. A leader must possess a keen and thorough self-awareness through an honest self-evaluation.

This self-evaluation should be on-going, motivated by agreed-upon goals. Lawrence Appley, author of *Values In Management* and other books on the same subject, has put it this way: "The real measure of the effectiveness of leadership at all levels is what is actually happening to the individuals directly responsible to that leadership, what changes are really taking place in the climate of the workplace, in the caliber of the people, and in the relationships of supervisor and supervised." That is how a leader's ability is assessed.

A leader must be the kind of individual who is able to manage many facets of the followers' lives. A good leader not only manages people, but also helps them deal with their problems, at work and sometimes in their lives away from work. And a good leader must also manage ideas that come from the people under her leadership.

This does not imply that a good leader steals the ideas that others have proposed. Rather, it means that a good leader is able to *manage* those ideas. Stop, look and listen to the ideas being offered. Discuss them thoroughly with the ones who proposed them. Analyze the ideas for their potential impact on the organization. A good leader asks, "Is it needed, practical, workable and cost effective, and will it achieve the desired result? Importantly, is it consistent with the organization's values?" If it is, then the leader's responsibility is to make certain that the ideas move forward and are implemented. And a good leader definitely makes certain that the originator of the ideas gets the credit – all the credit!

It is very important for a leader to acknowledge each of the ideas presented to him by his followers. Perhaps he cannot implement each and every idea presented, but acknowledgement of the idea and praise for the effort expended should be a prime order of business, one that is never denigrated or delegated to someone else.

Additionally, an effective leader needs to become a fount of knowledge. First, she must be able to read and understand herself. She must see herself as she is—warts and all—and as *others* see her.

Victorian poet, Robert Browning, offers this sage commentary on the human being, "O would some gift the giver give us, to see ourselves as others see us. It would from many a blunder free us, and foolish notion."

The leader must be able to step back, even as the artist steps back from his painting to examine the perspective, and view himself objectively. It is only then that he can recognize his strengths and weaknesses, vision, aspirations and the possible need for improvement.

A good leader must also know people. In general, he must be a student of mankind, and, specifically, he must know his own people. The leader must see the ins and outs, the comings and goings, the strengths and weaknesses, the interests, dreams and aspirations of his followers. Perhaps most importantly, he must have a sense of people's potential.

Additionally, a good leader must know the organization, its history, its products or services, its leadership, its rules and regulations, its benefits, and its mission or mission statement.

This is not where good leadership ends. A good leader must know the world. Followers live in the world outside the organization for 16 hours each day, 128 hours each week and 7000 hours every year. During these times away, followers are bombarded with world happenings that sometimes cloud their minds, and often implant negative ideas in their minds. In order to effectively partner with followers, the leader needs to be aware of what is going on in the world.

Last, but certainly not least, the leader must be a master of communication. She must know how messages get from Point A to Point B and back again. And she must know how to institute, manage, motivate and restructure the communication process and interaction. This is indeed a lofty challenge, and the effective leader will rise to it and be successful. Indeed, to be an effective leader is a daunting task. And yet, leaders are needed in every realm of human existence—family, industry, government and society.

As previously stated, effective leaders are. first and foremost, agents of change. They do what needs to be done to get the job completed efficiently and effectively. They are humane, sensitive, courageous, patient and ethical. They build trust that is imperative. They praise, lift and sometimes correct their in subordinates. A good leader is fair, impartial, visionary and dedicated to the ideal that each person is unique, has value, and possesses unlimited potential for success. It is only left for the leader to empathize, understand and help those individuals to achieve the highest level possible. As Abraham Maslow put it, "Man must be what he can be." It is the challenge and the responsibility of a leader to make that happen.

> *He who leads doesn't always wear a crown.*
> *It's hard to wash another's feet unless you're kneeling down.*
> *– Jim Mayfield –*

Application of V.A.L.U.E.S. to Leadership

Once you have made the commitment to leadership, beyond just accepting the role of leader, it is time to apply the process of *Communicating with V.A.L.U.E.S.* to your responsibilities.

Let's take a look at a fictional example:

Sam Mancuso, CEO of Bernhardt Publishing Company in Vreeland, Florida, is reporting to work on Tuesday, October 16. As he is walking down the hallway toward his office, he notices that Marjorie Dawson, the company's personnel director is in her office. Sam stops by and greets her.

> "Good morning, Marge. You know, coming to work early sure helps us beat the traffic, doesn't it?"
> "Yes, it does," she replies, but not with the normal lilt in her voice that people at Bernhardt have come to expect.
> "Marge, I just want to tell you how much I appreciate the good job you did in teaching the orientation class to our new people last Monday. Pete said that even after his six years with this organization, he learned things he didn't know—or had forgotten—

about the company. He also said that you not only gave good information, but that everyone walked out of the class laughing, and yet, invigorated, ready to tackle the world. Great job, Marge."

"Thanks, Mr. Mancuso, uh, Sam."

"How are things going for you right now, Marge?

"Okay, I guess. They're going pretty well."

"You don't sound too sure about that. Is there something you want to talk about?"

"I'm having a bit of a problem understanding and feeling good about the performance reviews that are coming up next month."

"What kind of problem? Do you want to talk about it?"

"I think they're too rigid, too demanding and too negative for anyone to get a real picture of a person and how he or she is performing."

"Really? I haven't heard that before. Tell me more."

"Well, it seems to me that most of the items on the report forms are looking for failure rather than accomplishment. It just seems kind of negatively skewed. Do you understand what I mean?"

"Well, sort of. I'd never thought much about it before, but maybe I should have. What do you suggest, Marge?"

"I really think the whole procedure for employee reviews needs to be studied and revised. I've got some ideas. I've been doing some research on review procedures, and I've been checking on how some other companies do theirs. Do you think we might be able to do something different?"

"I'll tell you what, this sets me thinking. You know the people in the company about as well as anyone. Why don't you pick four or five people, including yours truly, and we'll meet to kick this thing around. Oh, and be sure you pick someone from the real work force, and not just all us office bums. Give all of those you select some background material, if you can, so we can come somewhat prepared. Does that sound okay?"

"Can we do this pretty soon 'cause those reviews are coming up?"

"Yeah, Marge, let's make this an A Priority for early next week. Set everything up with Janie so she can schedule the room and stuff. And I'd appreciate it if you'd run the meeting. And, Marge, if we decide things need changing, we'll change them. I'm with you. Count me in."

"Thanks Sam, you're the greatest!"

"Likewise, Marjorie."

This fictional example is a case of leadership applying *Communicating with V.A.L.U.E.S.* Sam Mancuso greeted his personnel director, Marjorie Dawson. He valued (V) her by letting her know how much he appreciated the good things that she was doing. He asked (A) some good open-ended questions to bring her out. He noticed that she wasn't as chipper as usual, and he was concerned. He listened (L) to what she had to say. He then asked questions to make certain that he understood (U) what she was saying. He then empowered (E) her by authorizing her to select a committee to look at the problem. He also valued her by showing her that he trusted her judgment in the matter.

He did this instead of selecting the committee himself, or delegating it to his Vice President of Human Resources. He also made sure that there would be a breadth of representation on the committee. Sam also served (S) Marjorie by getting directly involved in the process. He assured her that he would stand behind any decision made by the committee.

This is one example of how the effective use of *Communicating with V.A.L.U.E.S.* can be for an organization. To give you a deeper look into *V.A.L.U.E.S.* we offer the following explanations.

V = *Valuing.* Our tendency is to value those things or people that give us pleasure and/or satisfaction. It is also our tendency to value that which we know best. We value our friends because we know them. We know their likes and dislikes, their joys and their sorrows, their peaks and their valleys, their successes and their failures, and, most of all, we know their potential and support them in their journey to reach it. We want the very best for them, and we want them to become self-actualized, the highest challenge and achievement of all.

If you are privileged to own a luxury automobile, you value it because you know it. You know the comfort it provides you, you know the safety devices it has, you know the pleasure you get from its powerful engine as you tool down the highway and you know its style and beauty. And you know how looking at it and riding in it makes you feel. You value your car because you know it well, and because of the pleasure and satisfaction it gives you.

If you are involved in some sport like bowling, you value it because you know it. Accomplished bowlers can usually remember a time when their bowling score began to improve, as well as the first time they threw three strikes in a row and when they achieved the highest score.

It does not matter whether you like bowling, gourmet cooking, needlepoint, fishing, golf, crafts, sailing or any other hobby or activity. You spend money on it, put time and effort into it, all because you place a value on it.

The point is: What we value, we invest in. Usually that investment comes in the form of our two greatest expendable resources, time and money.

Typically if you want to find out what people value, check their day-planner and checkbook.

As a leader, have you ever compared how you feel about your friends, car, hobby or recreational activity to how you feel about those people who answer to you on the job? Of course, they do not provide what the others give you. Sometimes they even give you a headache instead of a warm feeling all over.

A good friend, Bill Jackson, who does a lot of training in hospitals and healthcare organizations, tells a story about doing a leadership training session for a group of physicians. He was talking about valuing people with whom you work.

A physician, who practiced at a couple of clinics, leaned over to his office manager and said, "I think I do a pretty good job of valuing our people." She said, "You think so? Then tell me the names of the receptionists at our different locations." He realized that valuing his people meant interacting with them on a personal level.

The real question you should ask yourself is, do you know your employees as well as you know your car, your friends, your hobby, your family or your recreational activity? Perhaps this would be a good time to reread Chapter One on Valuing. The truth is you can only value what you know. And the place to begin valuing and loving is with yourself.

Review the list of roles in which you serve, and review the values you hold dear to see if they are directing you along the right path in your leadership position. Consider which of your roles gives you the greatest satisfaction. Which of your values do you believe has the greatest impact on your life and on your job? The exercise of examining your values requires that you consider where you spend your money, time, efforts, thoughts and actions. Ask yourself, "Do I spend all my time, energy and resources on people, projects, and actions that exclusively bring me pleasure and personal satisfaction, or do I spend some significant time and effort in bringing out the best in people for no particular personal gain?"

Think of the satisfaction you get from other people, and think of the feelings you have for employees who answer to you. Are you just putting up with them? Do you appreciate their efforts, as well as their accomplishments? Do you spend quality time and energy telling them so? Do you spend quality time learning more about their private lives? How much do you know about their families, hobbies, likes, dislikes, beliefs and personal problems? When you answer these questions, you will have a better idea of how much value you put on those whom you supervise or direct.

Consider again the heroes mentioned in Chapter One. For example, remember the man who died trying to save others in the Potomac River, or the Chicago man jumped into the river to try to save a drowning boy. You might not have an opportunity to extend yourself that far, but think about a recent problem experienced by one of your employees. Project your thinking a bit. What if the problem was potentially life threatening? Imagine that there was no solution to the problem, and the employee was going to die. How far would you go to help the employee solve the problem? How much time and effort would you expend to see that the problem got solved? Now, measure the distance between what you might do in the life-threatening situation and what you actually did to help the employee solve the actual problem. This reflection can help you determine the value you place on people.

Consider the concept of the servant-leader. Reread the poem, *The Servant-King* at the beginning of Chapter VI. Measure your own leadership by this model. Are you found where your employees are located? Are you available when they need you? Do you listen to them when they speak to you? As a leader, it is important for you to decide whether there are wide gaps between you and your people. Are there impenetrable obstacles blocking the path to your door? If there are, maybe now is the time for you to start closing that gap and removing those barriers.

Maybe Kenneth Blanchard could write still another book in his "one-minute" series. He could call it, *"The One-Minute Value and Praise."* That's all the time it takes to value, respect, honor and praise a person. Love is more than a word that describes a feeling. Love is also a verb that describes action. It is an action word. When you value another person, you are expressing your love for them. That is meeting their need for "self-actualization."

One of the most basic and meaningful ways to value people is to know and use their names. I'm sure trade people who know your name and actually use it have impressed you.

I have used the same dry-cleaners for 17 years. During the most recent three-year period, the same desk clerk always handled my dry cleaning. I frequented the cleaners at least twice a month, and every time I came into the establishment, the clerk would ask me my name. Early on, I asked her name and from then on I greeted her with a smile and used her name. She never caught on. Finally in disgust, I said to her, "Do you think it is important to remember people's names that you deal with on a regular basis?" Her reply was, "It certainly is. When I go to the grocery store or bank I expect them to know my name." As amazing as it is, the desk clerk had no clue. She was just repeating what society had taught her, not what she practiced.

Something as simple as taking the time to learn a person's name shows them that you value them. I suspect that a great number of people would agree on the value of knowing and using someone's name; yet, in business, I have found few people who use people's names with any regularity. In Dale Carnegie's first book, *How to Win Friends and Influence People*, he wrote, "A man's name is the sweetest sound in any language."

Consider the leadership in your company. How many of them know the name of every person who answers to them? How many of them know the names of the husbands and wives of their employees? A person's name is the badge they wear that identifies their uniqueness. It is what gives them individuality. A person's name is what sets them apart from their father, grandfather and great-grandfather.

Among adults of all walks of life, the inability to remember names is a source of embarrassment. "Your face is familiar, but I just can't remember your name." In meeting someone for the second time, you duck your head and turn away mumbling something like, "Mr. Mftt——," or you simply withdraw from making social or business contacts. Withdrawal because you cannot remember names tends to be detrimental to your business health.

There is an old adage, "To win a friend, you must be a friend." How long would your friendship last if you constantly called your best friend by the wrong name? Calling someone by his or her name helps to cement the relationship and shows that you care enough to remember their name. When you fail to remember and use a person's name, you are really saying, "You didn't impress me enough when we met for me to remember your name." Whatever your preoccupation at the time of meeting someone, if you cannot remember their name at your next meeting, it certainly suggests disinterest. If you are not interested in them, how can you expect them to be interested in you?

As is true with all deliberate remembering, the art and science of remembering names begins with attitude. You must want to remember the names of the people you meet. I have read more than once that the reason we cannot remember someone's name is that we did not get it in the first place—our minds were elsewhere when we were being introduced.

We will probably never match the name remembering ability of Napoleon Bonaparte. It is reported that he knew the names of every one of the thousands of officers that served under him. And we probably will not come close to the Greek Themistocles, who knew the names of 30,000 citizens of Athens. And yet, as business leaders, we owe it to our people to know their names.

Here is a process that I use to remember names. I call it the H.E.A.R.S.E. System®.

H = Hear

E = Echo

A = Attach

R = Remark

S = Spell

E = Exit

- **H** = Hear. Make sure you hear the name. The biggest reason we do not remember names is that we do not hear them to start with.

- **E** = Echo. Repeat the name back in a sentence. "John, it is great to meet you."

- **A** = Attach. Find a way to attach the name to a mental image. If you meet a person named Rose, picture a rose in your mind, and it will be easy to attach the name to the person.

- **R** = Remark. Make a remark about the name. If appropriate, make a positive remark about the name. For example, "Mary, I love that name, that was my grandmother's name." (Only if it is true, of course.)

- **S** = Spell. If it is an unusual name or one that can be spelled a couple of different ways, ask them to spell their name for you. (Do not use this as a lame attempt to recall the name.)

- **E** = Exit. Use the person's name as you exit. "John, great to talk to you. I will see you again soon."

If you are serious about improving your ability to remember names, it will take some work and focus. Firstly, practice when you meet a group of people. After you have met them, look at each one of them and recall their name. Secondly, get a "baby name" book. Go through the book and beside each name, write what picture comes into your mind as you hear that name.

A name like Rose is easy. Make your picture the same every time for that name. For instance, if your picture for Carl is a car, Use the picture of a car to attach the name to every Carl you meet. You will be amazed at how well this works. You only need to put the name into your short-term memory. If you focus on being better at names, you can improve. Calling people by their given name is a great way to value them. Get into the habit!

Marcus Buckingham and Curt Coffman wrote the landmark book *First Break All the Rules: What the World's Greatest Managers Do Differently*[8] based on in-depth interviews with over 80,000 managers in 400 companies. Buckingham and

Coffman offered a concept that all corporate leaders need to consider, "People leave managers, not companies. So much money has been thrown away in an attempt to keep good employees—in the form of better pay, better perks and better training—when, in the end, turnover is mostly a manager issue. If you have a turnover problem, look first at your managers."

If you look closely, you might discover that one of the major reasons for managerial failure is that the leader does not value employees in a way that is evident to them.

A = Asking. Certainly if a classroom teacher failed to ask the right kind of questions to her students, not much learning could take place. The teacher would not know where the students stood on the issues discussed or reviewed in the class. The teacher certainly would not know whether or not the teaching had been effective or when to move forward to challenge the students and help them grow academically.

It is not any different in the corporate world. If you want to know what is going on and/or where your employees stand on issues, rules and procedures, you have to ask questions!

Successful leaders decide they are going to ask questions. And then they decide what kinds of questions need to be asked. If you ask the wrong questions expecting the right answers, you are probably going to be disappointed with the results.

Consider once again the quote from David R. Hawkins, "Slight errors in the formation of questions result in gross errors in the answers that follow." When leaders ask the right kinds of questions, they can be pretty much assured of valid responses. This will certainly add strength to the communication relationship. Good questions lead to good conversation, which leads to effective problem solving.

One of the great points about asking questions is that,

except in extreme cases of open hostility, you *will* get an answer. Of course, it is possible you might not get the answer you are expecting or the answer you want, but you will more than likely get an answer.

Sometimes it is helpful to have a process when attempting to acquire a particular personal skill. Using acronyms helps our memory. For example, H.O.M.E.S. helps one remember the great lakes: Huron, Ontario, Michigan, Erie and Superior.

The same is true when trying to remember how to ask effective questions. An acronym like the one from Chapter Three, G.R.E.A.T. Questions© works wonderfully!

> *G*eneral question: How do you feel about the way things are going in your department?
>
> *R*elevant question: How do you feel the overall attitude is in your area?
>
> *E*xpectation question: Do you think this attitude is where we need it to be in order to be most effective?
>
> *A*dvantage question: If the attitudes in your department were where we wanted them to be, how would the company benefit?
>
> *T*ake-it-to-the-next-level question: Is your attitude where you want it to be?

Here are a few effective questions that can be used in with the G.R.E.A.T. Questions© formula.

- How do you feel about the project so far?

- What about this project is going well for you?

- What do you think is contributing to the success of the project?

- What do you need to complete the project that I might be able to get for you?

- What kind of support do you need to assure success?

- What results do you expect from this project?

- How can I help you get past the obstacle that is blocking you?

- What results would you expect if you reversed the process?

- What's next after you get the project completed?

- What are you looking forward to for tomorrow?

- What did you do today that you've never done before?

- What did you do today to make someone successful?

- What would you like to do again tomorrow that worked today?

- What else can I ask you that might prove helpful?

- How could you do that even better than you did today?

- What did you do today that deserves a pat on the back?

Of course, the questions you develop that move the communication process from a general question (G) to a take-it-to-the-next-level question (T) should be constructed to fit the situation. Just be sure the questions are current, direct and focused on the needs at hand.

Remember that asking questions is a wonderful way to build trust and respect. The law of reciprocity is at work. The fact that you asked someone's advice, feelings or input, suggests to them that you trust them, respect them and care what they feel and what they think. It then becomes easier for them to return the feelings and trust and respect you. What more could you ask?

Consider the person to whom you want to pose the question. Predict how they might respond. Phrase the question in a clear and concise manner, making sure it does not sound threatening or offensive. Questions can be effectively used in the business environment to produce interactive give and take.

In general, questions are used to get desired information, pass on information, determine another's feelings about a subject, get someone involved, enhance a relationship, help improve another's self-image, reach agreement, build trust and good will or be friendly and courteous. All of these reasons can be positive ways to meet the needs of the individuals involved, while also meeting the needs of the corporation.

If you want a short answer, maybe just a *yes* or a *no*, ask a close-ended question. If you want further dialogue with the person, ask an open-ended question.

The open-ended question is used to elicit ideas, concepts or feelings. Use the open-ended question when you desire more than a cursory response.

Regardless of the type of question you ask, just make sure you're asking for the kind of response you desire. Asking questions helps you learn what you do not already know. And asking questions is also an excellent means of breaking the ice with someone.

L = Listening. If asking questions is good, then listening for the response is even better. Most of a leader's day is spent listening. When you listen, you learn. When you *actually* listen, you honor the speaker. The quality of your existence is largely related to the quality of your listening. Whether you are at home, at church, at a service club luncheon or on the job, if you are an accomplished listener, you will enhance your own life while enhancing another's as well.

Listening helps us learn about products, services, people and purposes. It helps us build trust and rapport with others, and it certainly helps to put us in line for career growth.

Listening is a skill that can and should be learned. There are listening techniques, attitudes and concepts that can be taught and learned. With the right attitude, focus, determination and commitment, you can become a powerful listener and reap the benefits.

As stated in previous chapters, successful leaders cannot afford to pretend to listen. In fact, they need to be accomplished listeners.

Successful *listeners* must be able to overcome their negative feelings about the speaker, and they must not allow physical or psychological distractions to get in the way of their listening. Indeed, there are some barriers to effective listening that might seem insurmountable. And yet, a successful, listening leader has to put forth the energy required to break down any barriers.

Decide to be an active listener. This means listening with *all you've got*, being totally involved in the communication process—physically and emotionally.

Be an empathetic listener, in other words, listen from the speaker's point of view with a legitimate care for the speaker. An empathetic leader listens to the words spoken, the intensity of feeling, the emotional flavor, the power and the mood of the message. Listening expresses your leadership abilities and provides rewards in all aspects of leadership.

U = Understanding. To understand what we have heard requires knowing the person who's speaking. A successful, listening leader recognizes how the speaker accepts, internalizes, incubates and processes information, and he most likely has an idea of the employee's learning and behavior style.

When an employee has a particular experience on the job, the successful leader has some idea how the employee will use the experience in the future. The degree of success a leader has in knowing this depends on how well he knows the employee. When a leader knows even a little about the values, beliefs, goals and aspirations of another, he can be assured of gaining a better understanding of what the other person is saying and, sometimes, what is not being said.

As a reminder, being aware of the other person's social style from Chapter Four (Dominance, Influence, Steadiness, Compliance) can help you to in understand them. If a leader is aware of her employee's social style, it is possible for her to shift somewhat her own style in order to better relate to the employee. The social styles that seem to cover basic behaviors can be found in what has been called the DISC language.

D = Dominance. People who fall under this style of behavior are typically ambitious, forceful, decisive, direct, independent and challenging. At times they can even be overbearing and hard to get along with. They can be quick to get angry, but they rarely hold a grudge. Once something is over, it is over. They push hard to get things done, and they are not much for idle chit-chat. *Blunt* is a good one-word summary of their communication style.

I = Influence. This is the friendly persuader. Typically they are nice people who like others and enjoy interacting with them. They are good team players. They are optimistic, positive thinkers. *Coming up* roses is a good theme song for them. They tend to put their trust in others, sometimes without much thought or examination. They need a pat on the back regularly if they are to perform at their best. They do not make good poker players, because they cannot hide their emotions. If they get four aces, their eyes light up. They're impulsive and fun to be around.

S = Steadiness. People who fall under this style of behavior are steady and reliable. You probably will not hear any bragging from them. They just plod along, and they do it reliably. They do not get very excited, even when others around them do. They remain calm and relaxed. They stay pretty much to themselves, although they are ready to help you at a moment's notice. Even though they tend to be introverted, they will do just about anything to serve others. Unlike the *influencer,* those who are *steady* do not wear their feelings on their sleeve. They hide them, but make no mistake; they feel their emotions deep down inside themselves.

C = Compliance. People who fall under this style of behavior tend to be conservative. They do not jump to conclusions, and they are not quick to make decisions. They need to analyze, analyze and analyze some more. They like things neat and clean—well organized, if you please. They do not like to take chances or put themselves in a risky situation. When you deal with a person who has primarily a *compliance* style, you do not want to push them too hard, or they might break before bending. In the home, the wife who is a *C* will clean up after a party before she goes to bed, and her husband will have to put his dirty clothes in the hamper and not leave things on the floor. And he had better put the toilet seat down! And although the *C* is picky, picky, picky, he is very loyal and will stick with you to the end.

Each of the four social styles in the DISC formula is important to a well-run organization. You need someone to push hard sometimes to get a project done. You also need someone who is easy to be with and fun, speaks well, and has some positive influence on others. And there are certainly times when it is important to have a detail-oriented, conservative and exacting person involved in a project.

It is important to note that it is rare for one individual to be just *one* of these styles. All of us are a mix of these styles, but there is usually a predominant behavior characteristic by which each of us can be identified. It is that basic style you look for and adjust to as the leader. If you do this, your leadership will be more successful in getting your people to accomplish what needs to be done.

Intellectual understanding is, of course, critical to the success of any leader. We would hope that only the best and the brightest are in leadership roles. I think it goes without saying, a leader should be knowledgeable about our business, products or service. While we are not discounting the importance of having someone who is intellectually capable in a leadership position, knowledge or intellectual capacity alone is not the ruler that can be used to measure a successful leader.

Emotional understanding is a critical factor for success. Typically, the corporate world has placed most of the importance on intellectual understanding. *Emotional* understanding—EQ, as it is often called—is becoming a dominant force for understanding people. *Primal Leadership: Realizing the Power of Emotional Intelligence*[9], written by Daniel Goleman, Annie McKee and Richard Boyatzis, is an excellent resource on emotional intelligence.

Many leaders today are bringing specialists into their training programs to teach the concepts of emotional intelligence. As we discussed in an earlier chapter, EQ has been proven to be a very important predictor of success in employees.

Emotional intelligence is a part of an individual's nature

that allows her to understand, relate to, control, manage her emotions and recognize emotional responses in others.

This provides the successful leader with a much better chance of helping her followers achieve higher degrees of excellence. When a person is aware of her emotions, takes control of them, is aware of the intricacies of social connections and is able to manage her relationships on the job and in other important areas of her life, she can be said to be emotionally intelligent.

It is important for the successful leader to be aware of and in control of his emotions, as well as capable of building and maintaining strong, lasting relationships. With a high EQ, the successful leader is able to perceive the same elements in others and is better able to tolerate those he leads.

If your EQ is high, you will be miles ahead in the ability to empathize with others. It is your ability to empathize that opens the doors of understanding. Continue working on improving both your *intellectual and emotional* intelligence, because they both help you in your quest to understand others.

E = Empowering. Certainly one of the most important functions you have as a leader is to empower others. Giving a people power, providing them with the means to accomplish their tasks, helping them become competent and making dreams possible or easier to achieve are all examples of *empowering*. When you ask someone to do something great, and you show them you believe they can do what you suggest, you are *empowering* them. And when you support them through the entire process, you are definitely *empowering*.

When you discover the expectations held by one of your employees for a specific task or a major goal, you have taken the first step in helping them succeed. Nothing great ever happens without an expectation preceding it.

Desires come first, then expectations, followed by action.

It is a large part of the leader's responsibility to help her employees enlarge their expectations to achieve great results. Great results occur because of great expectations. Your people will tend to see themselves as less than what they are, with less ability to achieve what needs to be done. Often, they do this to protect themselves from failure. It is up to you to bring them up by empowering them with great expectations.

Until they have those great expectations, they will not do anything great. Do not be fooled by someone's false sense of satisfaction with the way things are going. When you invoke new and challenging expectations, you can rest assured that your employees will respond, often *beyond* your expectations.

Believe that there is nothing more honorable or productive than to empower others to bring out the best in themselves. Your respect for your people, and their respect for you, will grow exponentially as you empower them to become all that they can be.

When you evaluate your relationship with each of the employees who report to you, try to discover issus in their lives. You might find problems in their attitude, education, or motivation. Help them get rid of their, and see how far they can go.

We know that a person tends to become pretty much what he or she expects to become. A friend of mine is fond of saying, "Each and every person is exactly where they want to be. And if they are not happy, it's up to them to change." I'll change that last part and give you something great to do.

You can help people change by helping them change their expectations. Give them great challenges. Give them the power, the ability, the means and the authority to raise their expectations. Don't promise them the world—just empower them so that they can earn it for themselves.

S = Serving. We measure a true leader by observing how much he serves those he leads. Waving from your door won't do the job. Author and Minister Dr. Robert Schuler puts it this way, "Find a need and fill it, find a hurt and heal it." We might add, find an employee in your firm, discover a need they have and serve that person by helping them solve the problem.

Sometimes our own needs get in the way. When we really intend to serve others, we find that we are serving ourselves. This may be acceptable for some, but not for a leader. The definition of leadership is "a guiding or directing head." That refers to our guiding and directing others, not ourselves. Parents serve their children, often at the expense of their own needs. Heroes serve others, often at the expense of their own lives. Leaders serve their followers, even at inconvenience to themselves. They do it anyway, because that is what good leaders do.

One of the nicest benefits about serving others: it gets easier the more you do it. That could be because the rewards are so great. You feel terrific when someone you have helped succeeds in overcoming a problem or reaching a goal.

The effective leader finds the needs of his followers and discovers what can be done to meet those needs. The effective leader is a servant. This is how we recognize a true leader, when we see results in other people's lives.

Leadership Evaluation

For this exercise, finish the following sentence and place a check under the appropriate response below.

As a leader, I see myself as:

	Always	Not at all	Sometimes	Most of the time
Patient				
Kind				
Considerate				
A motivator				
A creative force				
An empowerer				
A communicator				
A team builder				
A role model				
A visionary				
A risk taker				
A coach				
Knowledgeable				
A quality controller				
Self-aware				
An encourager				
An implementer				
An idea manager				
An arbitrator				

CHAPTER 8

SELLING BEHAVIOR CHANGE WITH V.A.L.U.E.S.

Chapter by Carl Wickland
Executiv Director
American Probation and Parole Association

"All saints have a past. All sinners have a future." *Ancient Irish Toast*

C onvincing someone to change an attitude or a behavior that has been reinforced for years is not an easy task. Eliminating a lifetime of developed attitudes and learned behaviors is rarely, if ever, an instantaneous occurrence. Much has been written and documented about evidence-based approaches that can be implemented to help bring about attitude and behavior change. Techniques such as motivational interviewing and cognitive-behavioral approaches have shown great promise in helping people adapt healthier attitudes and pro-social behaviors. In many ways, getting someone to change an attitude or behavior is much the same as trying to sell someone a product or idea. After all, selling takes place in a variety of settings: parents selling life's lessons to their children around the kitchen table; teachers selling the value of learning to their students in the classroom; the minister, priest, rabbi or imam selling the attributes and rewards of living a spiritually driven life to their congregation; and managers selling leadership ideas to employees; and advocates selling a recommendation to a disgruntled judge, prosecutor, defense attorney or probationer.

Regardless of what one might be selling, whether it is

convincing someone to change their behavior, or getting someone to adopt a recommendation, you must have certain standards, characteristics, abilities and attitudes to be successful.

During a sales seminar for a major pharmaceutical company, participants were asked to describe the skills and attitudes of outstanding salespeople. Their responses were:

- Outgoing
- Perceptive
- Disciplined
- Balanced
- Honest
- Innovative
- Understanding of customer's needs
- Energetic
- Attentive listener

- Polite
- Resourceful
- Flexible
- Self-motivated
- Confident
- Persistent
- Knowledgeable about product
- Patient
- Sincere

These skills and attitudes were attributed to outstanding salespeople of a pharmaceutical company, however, with some minor adjustment, they are extremely relevant to the skills and attitudes needed to be successful in the corrections field. In a meeting of over 90 members of POPAI (Probation Officers' Professional Association of Indiana) the group was asked what skills make outstanding probation officers. Their list was identical to the sales list with the exception of "knowledgeable about product". This category could easily be "knowledgeable about the research and effective practices" or "knowledgeable about the probationer or parolee." "Hopeful" and "believes people can change" might be a couple of additions to the list. Nevertheless, this is a challenging list of attributes for any one person to possess.

As correction professionals, we are expected to be exemplary, perhaps even perfect. However, in other professions, less is expected. For instance, a 300 batter is considered good in any softball or baseball league in spite of the fact that the batter fails to hit the ball two out of every three times he or she is up to bat. Great bowlers have averages of over 200, not 300, which would be a perfect score. The top tennis players in the world do not serve an ace on every serve and rarely win a set without faulting on a serve. Attorneys who win two-thirds of their cases are in great demand by those who are accused of criminal activity. The most sought after surgeons in the world have lost patients during or after surgery. We know that such professionals in sports and other professions are not perfect, yet we consider them quite successful. In other words, no one is successful all of the time. While we hold ourselves to a high standard (check out the list above) we can never be all things to all people all of the time.

Being a successful correctional professional has more to do with internal characteristics, such as attitude, rather than "skills" of influence and research knowledge. To check this out, look at the previous list of characteristics of people's perceptions of a outstanding salesperson. You will note that nearly all of the characteristics reflect attitude, not skills and knowledge. What differentiates the outstanding correctional professionals from the ineffective ones is their attitude and emotional involvement.

While knowledge of the latest research, programs and products is critical, there are many correctional professionals who possess this of knowledge, but *do not* possess the unique qualities that could make them successful at bringing about changes in behavior.

Some people assume that once they are hired as a probation officer, correctional worker or similar position, and they are given a caseload or daily supervision responsibility, they have arrived at their destination. In reality, no one can be considered successful in corrections until they actually help someone change for the better. As in other facets of life, the title may suggest to others your *role*, but it cannot say anything about what you *do*. The title is assigned so that an opportunity is available. When you are hired and, perhaps after you graduate from pre-service training or an academy, the "diploma" you receive is the title *probation officer, correctional officer* or something similar that you receive. But this "graduation," just like in academia, is really just a commencement – a beginning.

The first, and probably most important, characteristic of an outstanding correctional worker is his or her attitude. That attitude must be one of wanting to helping people get what they want and need and creating value through building good relationships. For example, how many times have you walked away from a salesperson thinking, "I don't like her attitude?" The successful correctional worker needs an attitude of valuing others, a drive to succeed, and a positive outlook that can find the good in every person and situation. These are attitudes that have been proven to help people achieve greatness.

Have you heard people say, "You are a communicator. You would make a good (fill in the profession)?" In reality, there are people who seem to have natural abilities that help them communicate more effectively. That ability alone does not guarantee success in the corrections field. Successful people in the corrections field always deliver value and are focused on the needs of their clients – e.g. probationers, parolees, inmates, crime victims. They are problem solvers. We all know people like this in the profession. They manage to build value by giving their clients high priority and focusing on their client's needs even while being confronted daily by cynical and pessimistic attitudes and comments from their colleagues and the public.

Again, look at the previous list that distinguishes outstanding salespeople and, by comparison, outstanding correctional workers since much of what a correctional worker does is sell personal change. Qualities such as empathy, confidence, discipline, honesty and self-motivation are qualities that cannot be learned intellectually. They must be developed through experience and practice. Correctional workers attend numerous training programs throughout their careers that feature policies, procedures and practice considerations. Few programs focus on helping them develop the attitudes and skills that really separate the good from the great.

One of the key attitudes that outstanding correctional workers possess is persistence. Everyone with any time working in corrections has experienced the euphoria of finally getting through to someone on your caseload, only to have that euphoria leave because that same individual later commits a new violation or crime. It takes a special quality to not give in to the emotional roller coaster associated with unpredictability of human behavior. Correctional workers must have the persistence to accept that some degree of failure is a foregone conclusion. Most of the people you work with did not suddenly start making bad decisions one day, but instead honed their bad decision-making over years of experience. If you can't deal with the failure or the emotional pendulum of highs and lows that come with the job, a career in corrections is not for you.

"We must accept finite disappointment, but we must never lose infinite hope." - Dr. Martin Luther King, Jr.

Understanding that you are not always going to be successful is vitally important. Keeping an attitude of "I can" and "I will" will aid in getting things done. The people you are trying to help change *will* screw-up and they *will* do things that you should not or cannot tolerate. But you should not accept an attitude that you can't or won't work with them anymore. Successful correctional workers realize that things are not always going to go their way or work out. While they may be disappointed or frustrated with someone or something, they do not live their lives "under the circumstances." They are confident in themselves and their abilities, and, in the face of obstacles, they find a way to be successful. We see this same attitude in people who have achieved greatness in all walks of life.

Albert Einstein failed a math class, yet he became one of the greatest physicists. Helen Keller lost her sight and hearing at an early age yet she became a spokesperson and ambassador for the physically handicapped while providing motivation and assistance to thousands of afflicted people. Beethoven spent the last years of his life severely hearing impaired yet he wrote some of his best works during that period.

"It matters not what is behind or in front of us; what matters most is what is inside of us." – Ralph Waldo Emerson.

Behavior change does not take place unless there is a person willing to change. As a correctional worker, you need to sell the need to change. But the first sale you must make is *to yourself*. If you do not believe that the person can change, you are not likely to be successful. You need to believe change is possible or you are doing the client a disservice.

The second sale you have to make to a correctional client *is yourself*. You must build a relationship with the correctional client. If the client does not buy *you*, he or she probably will not buy your efforts to help them change. Building a good relationship is essential to any progress toward change.

How do you build a relationship with a client? You build it through what *you* do and what *you* say--by building trust and respect for *you*. If the client trusts *you*, believes *you* and respects *you*, he or she will more likely accept your direction, ideas and assistance. Show clients that you have integrity, honesty and respect for them by listening to them in order to understand their needs and issues. Communicate to them that you have a genuine interest in meeting their needs and to helping them move forward. If you can do this, you are on your way to a successful outcome.

During each interaction with clients, it is important to remember that whatever you say to them, how you communicate that you value them, what kind of questions you ask them, how well you listen to their response, how well you demonstrate that you understand their needs and how you empower them will determine what kind of relationship you will build with your clients. If you can do this well, then the relationships you have will be much more likely to be positive and successful.

Your role in selling behavior change must include building a relationship, helping convince the client of the need to change, and then, following-up to see how it is going. These three stages ensure that you will cement a positive working relationship.

A correctional worker needs additional qualities and characteristics to be successful. Some of these qualities are listed for your consideration.

Emotional Intelligence	Description
Self awareness	Getting to know your emotions.
Self management	Controlling those emotions.
Empathy	The ability to understand someone from his or her point of view rather than from your own.
Social expertise	The ability to build relationships.
Personal influence	The ability to motivate others
Social skills	The ability to facilitate and actively engage in communication.

A successful correctional worker also needs to possess a love for learning. There are those who assume that their learning, beyond on-the-job, lessens when they finish their academic education. It is essential that education be a life-long pursuit. To be a successful correctional professional, there should never be an end to learning even beyond the daily lessons that occur while on the job. There are new and effective approaches to your job that are chronicled in industry and academic publications as well as through training programs that are designed to increase your knowledge and improve your skills.

Constantly feeding your mind with new and challenging information stimulates your mind and keeps it sharp. Formal learning experiences, whether directly or indirectly related to your work, provide you with an expanded set of alternatives that include new mindsets and skills. New information and skills can assist you in determining if what you are doing is as effective as it could be. It is easy to go about your job as a correctional professional relying on only information you glean from your day-to-day experiences. These experiences can often be instructive. However, learning from the research, from others in the profession who ply their trade in different jurisdictions, and learning new skills is essential to being the most successful correctional worker you can be. Would you choose to go to a doctor who only learns from *practicing* medicine or would you choose to go to a doctor who also stays abreast of the latest evidence and procedures through formal education and journal articles? Community safety depends on your continual development as a professional.

It should be noted that successful correctional professionals have a healthy level of enthusiasm. Most people enter this field with the hope of making a difference in a crime victim's or probationer's/parolee's/inmate's life, and to make the world a safer and more peaceful place. Unfortunately, enthusiastic workers often run head-on into workers from their offices, or other justice professionals, who perpetuate cynicism, pessimism and apathy. Nevertheless, successful correctional workers must embrace positive energy whenever they can so that the energy is transferred to their clientele and other workers.

Work Ethic

Working in the corrections field is difficult and challenging. Furthermore, being a successful correctional professional requires ongoing skill development and enhancement. Enthusiasm and good intentions are not enough to effectively bring about behavior change with correctional clientele.

First, one needs to be well-versed in effective practices. This requires staying abreast of the latest research and attending training that presents information on evidence-based practices. It is essential that you add to your knowledge base and challenge your intuition by reading and learning about practices and policies that have proven to be effective in the field.

Second, you need to learn how to apply outstanding practices and skills to ensure you are performing your job at an optimal level. Throughout their careers, every successful athlete, surgeon, auto mechanic, etc. wants to learn new skills and update their techniques. They also seek to receive feedback on their proficient use of their new skills, usually before they institute the practice or skill in their daily endeavors.

Finally, to maintain proficiency with any skill, you have to practice it on a regular basis. Professional golfers hit hundreds of golf shots nearly every day to keep their game sharp. If you learn a skill such as motivational interviewing, it is important that you put that skill to use on a regular basis.

Outcomes

The outstanding correctional worker must also have a set of outcome measures that they are striving to meet or exceed. Success in corrections in not obtained by simply receiving a pay paycheck. The public wants, and expects, to be safe from harm by those that are in the corrections system and to see justice done. Thus, it is important to set (either alone or with others) outcome measures that gauge your success in such things as recidivism reduction or restitution collection. Beyond the "big picture" outcome measures, it is also a good idea to set daily or weekly goals so you can recognize short-term success in a job that often has many set-backs and requires extensive effort with each individual over a long period of time.

Planning

Successful people usually use their ability to plan ahead as one of their distinguishing characteristics. They do not live in the future, but they plan for the future while they work in present, to have things happen the way they have planned. Many correctional professionals have been schooled in the use of case plans that are developed with each person on a caseload. Much has been written about the importance of case plans and this publication is not going to get into the nuances of case planning. Suffice it to say regarding case plans, selling it to the client, and developing it with the client, is important to success. Of course, anyone who has worked in corrections knows that because it is a profession that focuses on the human behavior of individuals who are not known for making good decisions, the best laid plans often go awry and one incident can upset your carefully devised plans. Just because your plans don't work out on a given day, that doesn't mean it was a bad plan. Consider keeping the plan for another day or rewriting the plan to include necessary changes in circumstances. Here are a few simple guidelines to effective planning.

Write it down. There are several reasons for writing down your plans – which, by the way, is much easier these days with automated case management systems. First, you are more likely to remember the plan if you have taken the time to write it down. Second, because you likely have many daily distractions, it is easier to carry out the plan if you can read it back to yourself. Third, when you write it down, it becomes almost like a contract or a promise to carry out the plan. Fourth, with an automated case management system, reminders and activities can automatically populate the case file.

Make certain it's something the client really wants to have happen. If the person expected to accomplish the goals of a plan is not in agreement with them, it is unlikely you will have much success. Utilizing motivational interviewing (MI) techniques, and ensuring there are incentives for reaching a goal, will help ensure buy-in from the client. Much has been written about MI and part of the ongoing knowledge and skill development should include learning how to use MI techniques.

Make sure it is something you both can do. Do not develop a plan with strategies that require you to do the impossible or improbable. There are many activities in which you would like to be involved to ensure the best possible case plan outcome. Some of them are practical and can be accomplished, and some of them are simply not practical. Your failure to hold up your end of a case plan may be viewed as reason for the client not to complete his/her goals.

Give each goal a time limit. Setting a time frame in which a goal will be accomplished is essential to any case plan. It is wise to set short-term goals considering the impulsive nature of many correctional clients. Creating small steps for a larger purpose also sets up the opportunity for more positive affirmations.

Application of V.A.L.U.E.S. to Corrections

If you have made the commitment to work in corrections, it is assumed you have decided to be the best correctional professional you can be. It is time now to see how *Communicating with V.A.L.U.E.S.* can be applied to your everyday communications with clients, co-workers and others.

This process is called *V.A.L.U.E.S. Communication*

V – Value – Establish rapport, make an emotional connection, respect the individual

A – Ask – Pose G.R.E.A.T. questions that create further understanding

L – Listen – Actively develop empathy and build trust

U – Understand – Connect with the messenger and the context of the message

E – Empower – Provide opportunities to generate self expectations and tolerate self- determination

S – Serve – Suspend own wants to help meet another's needs

Presented below is a simplified and somewhat elementary scenario that is meant to be illustrative of *V.A.L.U.E.S. Communication.* Not all of the preliminary communications are represented in this scenario and some of what would need to happen is assumed to have happened. The time sequencing is also accelerated.

Betty Jones, probation officer had a scheduled appointment to develop a case plan with Tom Smith, a new probationer. After an initial greeting and introduction, they sat down in Betty's office. Tom Smith immediately stated in a gruff tone, "All right, tell me what I gotta do."

Betty responded, "Before I do that Mr. Smith, may I ask you a few questions?"

Tom: "Yeah, I guess so. I gotta be here anyhow."

Betty: "What activities do you have going on in your life at this time Mr. Smith?"

Tom: "I got work five days a week, I play softball two nights a week and I have to keep up around the house and spend time with my boy. Now I have to go to drug treatment and do community service work."

Betty: "Wow, you certainly do have a full plate of activities. Have you given any thought to how you might meet all of these responsibilities while leaving some time for your son, relaxation and some fun? In other words, how will you maintain your current responsibilities and activities with the addition of your probation conditions?"

Tom: "I don't see where I can have any time to do every-thing with all that I have to do. I really don't know how I can do it all."

Betty: "Mr. Smith, it sounds like you are feeling a little overwhelmed by what you are expected to do. I do expect you to maintain your employment, see to your family duties and successfully complete those activities the court said you had to do. But...I don't expect all of those things to get completed all at the same time or get completed by tomorrow. Should we try to prioritize your activities so you don't get overwhelmed but still complete what you are expected to complete?"

Tom: "Yeah...okay. By the way, you can call me Tom"

Betty: "OK Tom, will you tell me what you feel your pri-ority activities should be at this time?"

Tom: "I gotta work so I can keep a home and have food on the table for my wife and son. Also, the insurance I get at work will help pay for some of my drug treatment. So work would be my top priority. Without work, everything else will fall apart."

Betty: "I think we both can agree that work is certainly one of your top priorities and you need to maintain your job. I also have heard you say that your family is important to you. What else would be a priority for you?"

Tom: "I dunno. I sure don't want to have to go to drug treatment."

Betty: "Tom, haven't you had problems at work in the past because of your drug use? Will you tell me what kinds of issues have come up at work that may be related to drug use?"

Tom: "Yeah...I got suspended once, missed a few days and they are telling me that I need to stop using drugs."

Betty: "How would not addressing your drug use get in the way of you keeping your job?"

Tom: "Well, given the crime I committed and the court saying I have to complete drug treatment, my work is going to be watching me closely to see if I do what I'm supposed to do. I think this is my last chance to keep my job."

Betty: "How will drug treatment get in your way?"

Tom: "It will probably keep me from getting to play soft-ball which is where I have some non-drug using friends."

Betty: "Having friends that don't use drugs is important and I'm glad you recognize that. Tom, do you know for sure that the drug treatment sessions will interfere with all of your softball games? What options do you think you have so you can still play some softball? What are you will-ing to do to make sure you can fulfill your other expecta-tions?"

Tom: "Well, some of my games are on weekends, so, I could miss some games while I attend treatment but still play in other games. I guess you're right that maybe I need to cut-back some on softball and get through drug treat-ment so I don't have that hanging over my head."

Betty: "How has your drug use had a negative impact on your relationship with your family?"

Tom: "They try to avoid me when I'm high. They act scared to be around me."

Betty: "How do you think they would react if you stopped

using drugs and worked your way off probation?"

Tom: "They would be proud of me. I would be proud of me. There would be less arguments and I would be a better dad."

Betty: "It sounds like there are some pretty good incentives for you to go to treatment. What other concerns do you have about going to treatment?"

Tom: "It will be too tough to do...that I will fail."

Betty: "Those are certainly legitimate concerns. It has been a long time since you have been drug free and it will be a big change. You just need to get started in the right direction. You have already gone several days without using drugs because of your time in jail. So...you are off to a good start. How do you envision your life if you are drug free?"

Tom: "I will either get promoted at work or find a better paying job that isn't so hard physically. I will be able to do things with my son and wife that I have missed because of being high. I will be able to live without having to look over my shoulder."

Betty: "That's a wonderful vision. What other concerns do you have besides the ones you shared about attending treatment?"

Tom: "I am concerned about all the stuff I have to do to make the judge happy. What about the community service work I have to complete? What if I slip up and have a dirty drug test?"

Betty: "I appreciate that you are feeling a bit overwhelmed by all the new expectations you have to meet. Regarding your drug use, let's get you enrolled in treatment first and then take it one day at a time regarding any future drug use. I want you to succeed. So, as for your community service work, what would you say to delaying the start of your community service work until after you complete the first stages of treatment. Then, you don't have too much on your plate at one time?"

Tom: "That would be great."

Betty: "To be clear…you still will be expected to complete your community service work before you are discharged from probation. I do want you to complete the community service work as does the judge, but I will write a note to the judge by the end of the week asking if we can delay your start so you can first focus on being successful in treatment while maintaining your job."

Tom: "Okay."

Betty: "So Tom, do we have a plan? Do you agree with what we both will do?"

Tom: "Yes we do. And, I do agree with the plan."

Betty: "Agreed. We have a plan and we'll monitor your progress together. For now, I expect that you will begin addressing the issues we have talked about and I will follow-up with the judge. So…Is there anything more you need me to do today to help get you started?"

Tom: "I'm a little nervous about treatment. Would you help me contact them to get started?"

Betty: "Sure Tom we can do that together. Let me get the number…"

Most people involved with the justice system that have been accused of, or have committed, a crime are usually not willing participants in the justice process. This makes the job of engaging these unwilling clients in behavior change activities through the use of *V.A.L.U.E.S. Communication* that much more difficult. For example, by the time probationers come in contact with a probation officer they have gone through several experiences with the court system: They have been arrested (hand cuffed and processed) by law enforcement; put into jail or holding cell where they are first questioned, searched and assessed; made several court appearances; had to find money for an attorney or engage with an attorney they didn't choose but had assigned to them; and many other possible scenarios of being processed through "the system." The probationer also has had little control over the process. In short, they are demeaned and devalued through actions and processes. It is, therefore, important from the onset to develop a relationship that will yield positive outcomes.

Threats and intimidation are not effective strategies to bring about long-term behavior change. A more effective way to "sell" someone on change is first through the establishment of rapport and showing respect ("V" of *V.A.L.U.E.S.*). Betty did this by being polite, asking Tom's permission to proceed and by letting him know that she knew probation was not going to be easy.

Betty relied on inquiry, "A", rather than edicts or demands. She asked primarily open-ended questions that empowered Tom to have some control over the direction of the conversation. By feeling empowered, Tom is more likely to take ownership for future actions resulting from their meeting.

Betty also made a point of listening, the "L," to Tom's answers and the concerns he voiced as he expressed what was important to him. She responded to him by repeating what he said so he knew she understood. She expressed empathy for his concerns and recognized his challenges. A word or two on listening--effective and active listening is one of the most important skills for a correctional professional. This skill can help discern unspoken objections or fears. Learning to listen empathically – listening from the client's point of view – will give you emotional knowledge about the client rather than only facts and observed behaviors. Possessing this knowledge, and utilizing it, in your work will help ensure positive relationships with successful outcomes.

Betty clearly understood what Tom was communicating to her, the "U." She also gave Tom the opportunity to develop some of his own solutions, the "E," when she addressed his desire to continue to play softball. And she made the meeting about Tom and what he needed to do and how she could help him, the "S".

Betty also used the G.R.E.A.T. Questions system of asking questions. Let's review how this was accomplished:

General question: "May I ask you a few questions?"

Relevant question: "What activities do you have going on in your life at this time Mr. Smith?"

Expectation question: "What options do you think you have so you can still play some softball? What are you willing to do to make sure you can fulfill your other expectations?"

Advantage question: "How do you think they would react if you stopped using drugs and worked your way off probation?"

Take-it-to-the-next-level question: "How do you envision your life if you are drug free?"

Betty ended the session with her offer to call the treatment program with Tom before he left. Getting Tom to enroll in drug treatment was one of the main objectives of the meeting.

In the case above, Betty didn't directly express how she valued Tom. However, she did effectively express her good intentions by asking permission to ask questions. This suggested to Tom that she valued his input and that she was willing to consider what he wanted instead of just telling him what he had to do.

Valuing comes in many forms. The scenario did not have Betty complimenting Tom on being on time or how good it was to see him in street clothes rather than a jail jumpsuit. Betty did focus on asking pertinent questions, listening, understanding, empowering and serving Tom. In short, Betty was valuing Tom by how she conducted herself in the interview.

It is easier to value a correctional client when you have done your homework. Having background information about the person's circumstances beyond the immediate offense will provide a better chance for you to show that you value of the individual, thus making the line of questioning can be more relevant and thoughtful.

We can be expected to have greater understanding when we know more about the person who is speaking. If you find you are hindered in your understanding, then it is prudent to return to asking good questions. It is important to know that the meaning of what is being said to you is actually what you understand it to be. If you are unsure, ask questions! The question unasked is rarely, if ever, answered.

For most educated people, intellectual understanding is fairly commonplace, however, sometimes emotional understanding, even for highly educated and intelligent people, can be difficult to develop. Facts are easier to digest and relate to than abstractions of subjective sensations. In order to understand – or at least appreciate – another person's emotions, it is necessary to understand and accept your own. When you are aware of your own emotions, have them contained, are cognizant of social forces, and know how to manage them to build strong connections with others, it is much easier to understand and gauge other people's emotional capacities. It should be stated that being aware of your emotions is not the same thing as being able to define emotions. Emotions, by their very nature, are abstractions of guttural manifestations based on a conglomeration of experiences that may emanate from deepest pockets of one's subconscious. In short, emotions are felt and displayed, but rarely well-defined. Nevertheless, gaining a handle on a correctional client's emotional condition is vitally important to improving your ability to empathize with and appreciate their view of the world. Effective correctional professionals also are able to empower their clientele by asking questions that solicit attitudes, feelings and opinions which will aid in moving the client toward a successful result.

Finally, it is important to end any meeting with a correctional client similarly to how a good salesperson would end a sales call. You must "close the deal"--the client must commit to specific action. Consider Betty's meeting with Tom. It was not enough to merely talk about Tom's needs and then only discuss how he might be able to meet those needs. Betty's effectiveness is in her ability to skillfully use the VALUES process to honestly and purposefully connect with Tom, and then to lead him to see the value in committing to a course of action that he recognizes will benefit his life and future. Likely, all would have been for naught if Betty had ended the session with, "If you decide you want to do these things, give me a call." A good close has the following elements: Agreement of need; clarity of purpose; and execution of the next step.

Barbara Broderick, Chief Probation Officer for Maricopa County Adult Probation and former APPA President wrote, "In our work, we need to build trust and develop understanding before we can effectively engage others in problem-solving and change." Developing the ability to skillfully use the VALUES communication tools presented here will assist you in being an outstanding correctional worker who effectively builds that trust and understanding; it will equip you to be a force for positive change with your clients and in your community.

CHAPTER 9

CUSTOMER SERVICE WITH V.A.L.U.E.S.

> Managing an organization's human resources equates with managing its customer services. Employee relations equals customer relations. The two are inseparable.
>
> *Robert Desatnic, Managing to Keep the Customer*

S imply open a magazine, turn on your television, read the Sunday newspaper, drive along our highways and listen to your car radio. What do you see and hear? The result of billions of dollars spent on advertising, with the express purpose of soliciting new customers for products and services. Company A is willing to spend 100 million dollars to advertise their product, but denies or delays a customer's request to have their gadget replaced or repaired at a cost of $25.00! How foolish of them, considering that it costs as much as five times more to secure a new customer as it does to maintain an old one.

Stranger still is that many companies that fail to value their regular customers, actually spend outrageous funds to gain new ones, often making promises of quality, delivery, replacement, repair and service that they fail to keep, or keep but with hesitant response.

Companies who consistently make this mistake not only lose their customer to a customer-oriented competitor, but the other nine or ten potential customers to whom that former customer speaks. This raises the cost of poor customer service even higher. The following tables show how much dissatisfied customers can cost a hospital.

Hard Costs

Dissatisfied patient	1
Assumed revenue associated with a typical hospitalization	$24,000.00
Assumed average number of hospitalizations in the patient's remaining lifetime	x 5
Total *	<u>$120,000.00</u>

Soft Costs

Dissatisfied patient	1
Additional patients with a significant, *unspoken* complaint	<u>+ 6</u>
Significant patient complaints	7
A dissatisfied customer typically tells nine to ten people of their dissatisfaction	x 9
People eventually hearing negative word-of-mouth reports about the hospital	63

* *Published by AHRQ with HCUP data, Feb. 2009*

Let's assume that one-forth of the 63 people are influenced by the negative *word-of-mouth* to the degree that they seek hospitalization elsewhere. And let's use the hard cost total for the analysis above in order to develop an indication of the potential opportunity costs.

Opportunity Costs

People receiving negative *word-of-mouth*	63
Assumed level of influence	x <u>5</u>
People choosing to be hospitalized elsewhere	16
Previously determined hard costs	x <u>$120,000</u>
Potential lost revenue *	<u>$1,920,000</u>

Formula used from
<u>Source: Healthcare Financial Management December 1989</u>

Major necessary services and products such as telephone, medical facilities, department stores, grocery stores, pharmacies, restaurants, automobiles, real estate firms, electronic firms, office supply companies, carpet cleaners, trade schools, etc., have few differences in their products or services from one firm to the other. In most cases, cost differences are inconsequential. Location is usually not a problem. Product displays are basically similar. Product differences are generally minimal and, as in the case of department stores and electronic retail outlets, the products are basically identical.

How does a consumer make the decision on which company to choose when purchasing its goods or services? Customer service is the one difference that consumers can *feel* and *talk about* with family, friends, neighbors and co-workers. Make no mistakes, consumers can, and will, talk about it. That is why companies that train employees in good customer service will not only remain on the scene longer, even during tough economic times, they will make a higher net profit, as well.

Some companies that employ **customer service representatives** tend to hire the youngest, most _in_experienced applicants and often pay them the lowest wage in the company. This is akin to paying teachers—who have the responsibility to teach future doctors, lawyers, engineers, scientists and business executives—some of the lowest professional salaries in our nation. A company's economic future rests in these inexperienced and low-paid **customer service representatives.** A company's economic health rests on the success of the customer service program it promotes.

In addition, some **customer service representatives** are often considered second-class within their company. If they are fortunate, they occupy a cubicle the size of a toilet stall. Many do not even have a cubicle, and must muffle their conversations with customers so as not to disturb their colleagues, sitting one foot on either side of them. And unfortunately, most customer service representatives have so little authority that they must get every decision approved by their manager. This is probably due, in part, to the fact that they are so poorly trained for their job and not valued or trusted by their management.

If that is not bad enough, there is something that is even more troubling than untrained, underpaid, inexperienced and low-authority customer service representatives. Often customer service is separated from the rest of the firm. It is a separate entity, and often is undervalued by the rest of the organization. It is indeed rare that the entire workforce of a company has been trained in the importance of customer service.

Any company, regardless of its product or service, should include a substantial training segment on customer service during its new employee orientation program. Each new employee should come to realize that her job depends on customer satisfaction.

Of course, if customer service is to be a focus in any company, it has to be valued. Every leader in the firm has to speak of it, believe in it and commit to it. All employees must become customer-service oriented, because all employees have contacts *outside* of the company.

Consider this, "we are what we believe, we believe what we are taught, and then we become a part of it." If *customer service* is a part of our daily vocabulary, others around us will hear about it. If a company has top leadership committed to customer service and to customer service training for all employees, you can bet that their customers know it, feel it and tell others about it. The results will be evident at the bank in the bottom-line profits!

So very often, a company examines its policies and procedures after a problem occurs, but rarely when all seems to be going well. It might prove helpful to see positive results from your effective customer service program. Many companies that are interested in customer service employ an outside firm to measure customer satisfaction. The one question that most people agree is the most important in a survey is: "Would you recommend this company or product to your family or friends." The answer to this question will pretty much determine the quality of customer service a company is providing.

Another benefit of a customer survey is that when customers receive outstanding service they report it to the company's management. A customer service survey is a vehicle to encourage more customers to praise good service. And the wise manager knows that praise for good customer service is most valuable when this praise gets back to the person or persons responsible for the positive results. Some firms have award or bonus programs for those who enhance the company's reputation for customer service. It is even a good policy to let all of your employees know what happened, when it happened and who provided the good service. This is something that is worthy of being placed in the company newsletter, posted on the bulletin board or sent out through e-mail.

We know that employee relations mirror customer relations. Some studies indicate that for every two point gain in employee satisfaction, there is a one point gain in customer satisfaction. The two are inseparable. You never treat your customers any better than you treat your coworkers. This is a vital point that each and every company should heed. Certainly, if a company has poor employee relations, its customer service suffers as a result. If employees are not valued, trusted, involved, enriched, trained, paid adequately, supported, listened to, empowered and respected, management cannot expect the customer to be treated any differently. Customer service can be a reflection of employee relations.

Application of V.A.L.U.E.S. to Customer Service

A number of years ago, the executive of a Swiss manufacturing company was traveling with his family near Innsbruck, Austria. He was driving his Rolls Royce Silver Shadow when he hit a large pothole on a mountain road and broke the front axle. He managed to have the car towed into town. He contacted, via the international toll-free telephone number, the Rolls Royce customer service department, and they flew a technician and a new axle to Innsbruck the next day.

The car owner knew he had no warranty remaining, so he waited for two months for a service and repair bill from Rolls Royce. Finally, he called the company and asked for the bill. The customer service person assured him there was no bill outstanding. He informed the person on the telephone that it was for a broken axle replacement.

The service person said this to him in reply: "Sir, Rolls Royce axles do not break. Thank you for calling, and have a pleasant day."

This is customer service at its best. Can you imagine the Swiss gentleman ever bad-mouthing Rolls Royce? Not hardly!

Let's apply the process of V.A.L.U.E.S. to customer service. The first step is (V) Valuing. A *customer service representative* can begin with a simple "Thank you for calling. How may I help you?"

This opening also includes the (A) Asking step of the process. The caller has been valued by hearing "Thank you for calling" and has been asked a general question, "How may I help you?" Depending on the customer's response, the *CSR* can then ask pertinent questions for clarification in order to be certain of the problem. He can also ask for specifics if it seems advisable or necessary.

And then, the *CSR* can listen, listen and listen some more. This is the (L) Listening step in the process. It is key to helping solve the problem, and it enhances the act of valuing the person.

It is also imperative that the *CSR* understands the problem from the customer's point of view. This is the (U) Understanding step of V.A.L.U.E.S. Even if the customer is upset, argumentative or irrational, it is important for the *CSR* to remain calm and in control of the communication process. She can do this best by assuring the customer that she understands that there is a problem and that her job is to get to the bottom of it so the problem can be solved.

The (E) step of Empowering is to make certain that the customer never feels that he is powerless in the situation or of little or no value to the company.

It helps if everyone understands how to handle a problem with a customer. The focus should always be on solving the customer's problem, while staying within the guidelines of the company. Is the customer always right? I suspect not. Sometimes, for various reasons, customers can make unrealistic demands and set unreasonable expectations. They may even become emotional and difficult.

However, we should recognize these times as *opportunities*. Studies have shown that customers whose problems are solved to their satisfaction become more loyal. First, neutralize the emotion, and then you can focus on the problem to create a win-win situation.

All "IZE" on the Customer

Use the following logical approach to solve customer or people problems:

Apologize

Empathize

Analyze

Formalize

Finalize

Summarize

Apologize. Many times all a customer wants is for someone to listen and care that they have a problem. In his excellent book, *Patient Satisfaction, Defining, Measuring, and Improving the Experience of Care*, Dr. Irwin Press[11], in talking about studies of malpractice claims in healthcare says, "All studies of malpractice claims show the same result. Communication is the key to the vast majority of suites. Anger, not injury, is the trigger for most claims."

There is a science to apologizing. First, never follow "I apologize" with "but." When you say "but" you are turning your apology into an excuse.

Second, be careful about using implied, "It's your own fault, dummy" statements. "If you hadn't done _____, this would not have happened." The implication is that if you had acted right or had not done something stupid or dumb, this would not have happened.

Empathize. Empathy just says, "I understand that you have a problem, and I am sorry that you have that problem. Take note that, "I know how you feel" should only be used when it's a true statement. Otherwise you may offend the customer.

Empathy is about action more than words. It is proven in how we listen, our body language and our deeds. If we have empathy, our customers will sense it.

Analyze. Charles Kettering of General Motors fame said, "A problem well defined is half solved." The following questions are helpful to ask yourself as you are solving a problem:

1. Is this the problem or is it a symptom of a more serious problem?
2. Is it an on-going problem that needs to be solved at a different level?
3. Who can help me analyze this problem?
4. Who owns the solution to this problem?
5. What is my obligation to my customer? To my company?
6. How can I create a win-win situation?

Formalize. Henry Ford said, "An opinion of one is no opinion at all." Often, the best person to come up with the right solution is the person who has the problem, also called the *owner.* Simply by asking the *owner* what her expectations are, and how she would like to see the problem resolved, you may come up with an ideal solution. And as long as you are following the company's guidelines, you can try asking others who deal with similar problems how they have solved similar problems in the past.

Finalize. Make sure that solving the problem will not create new problems in other areas for other people. Sometimes problems can have a ripple effect. Look at the problem and the solution from all angles.

Summarize. Make sure you and the customer understand the solution to the problem. Nothing is worse than thinking you have solved the problem only to discover later that there is another misunderstanding. Always summarize the agreed upon action, and where prudent, have the customer sign an agreement that they are satisfied with the solution.

Working through this simple problem solving process (Apologize, Empathize, Analyze, Formalize, Finalize and Summarize) will help you to identify and formulate a plan that can solve your customer's problem.

Serving (S) the customer means that you take responsibility and ownership of the problem. It means following up to make sure the customer is satisfied.

CHAPTER 10

COACHING WITH V.A.L.U.E.S.

> "As a manager, any time you choose not to help your employees succeed, you are involved in self-destructive behavior."
> *Ferdinand F. Fournies, Coaching for Improved Work Performance*

A coach's job is to help others reach their potential and to see more in others than they see in themselves. Think of the people in your life who may have helped and encouraged you. Maybe it was a parent, a teacher, a friend. Someone who coaches isn't always called a coach.

Learning to coach is a vital skill in the marketplace today. With the cost of turnover, and the well-stated point by Jack Welch that "employees leave managers, not companies", leaders *must* learn to coach. Consider the following: With training you get compliance, with coaching you get commitment. Of course, we all know that commitment from our team members is much more desirable than mere compliance!

A coach is found in every profession, every sport, every skill, every family and every occasion where someone places his trust in another person to help them toward meeting their potential. A baby learns positive behaviors from his parent. A child learns to read, write and do math from her teacher. An aspiring baseball player learns how to catch a ball, how to hold and swing a bat, how to run the bases and how to take a loss as well as learn from it, from his coach. And an employee who is open, teachable, motivated and promote able, learns from others whom she trusts and respects.

Coaches are special kinds of people. They have special abilities, characteristics and methodologies for their coaching.

Although you might add to the list, great coaches have the following five traits:

- A servant's heart.

- A desire to help people succeed.

- A winning attitude.

- A commitment to excellence.

- The ability to foster trust.

Let's take a look at each of these five traits, one at a time.

A servant's heart. A great coach in any circumstance or situation, whether or not she is holding a position, title or special assignment, is definitely a leader. As we suggested in a previous chapter, a leader is one who gets things done through people and is one who serves those he leads. He must possess a servant's heart.

Kahlil Gibran expressed what could be a coach's motto in his book *The Prophet.* "The teacher…gives not of his wisdom, but rather leads you to the threshold of your own mind." *What* Galileo Galilei wrote can also be applied to coaching: "You cannot teach a man anything. You can only help him discover it within himself." This is why the coach must be a servant.

In communication, there is a *speaker* that brings a *speech* to an *audience.* The audience can consist of one or more persons. Regardless of the size, the audience is the most important element in the equation. A speaker must always be a servant to the audience, whether it is the President of the United States, a pastor of a congregation of 50 senior citizens, a coach of the Los Angeles Lakers, or a mother teaching her baby the meaning of the word "no."

John Thornby was a brilliant man. He was always able to see the *big picture* and stay focused on the task at hand. What made him great was his refusal to participate in anything in which he did not believe. John was the director of a major insurance company. The company was a highly charged political entity, comprised of a group of warring departments whose personnel seemed to be more interested in achieving their own ambitions than in making a profit for the company. What made Mr. Thornby so effective was that no matter how much sniping and pettiness existed around him, he always managed to rise above it, and remain uninvolved in the fray. There were those who tried to get John involved, but he refused to participate in the schemes that were so unproductive.

John Thornby had a servant's heart. He listened politely as people tried to get him involved with them. He went about the business of making his department successful by constantly helping his employees. People throughout the company wanted to work for John. He was respected and trusted. He had integrity. Above all, those who worked under him knew that he always put their needs and interests first. Even when the company was going through some tough economic times, John's department seemed to somehow meet its objectives. He spent his time building up, not tearing down, unlike so many of his fellow managers. He did this because he had a servant's heart.

Most corporate leaders have moved up in the ranks. This is certainly the rational way for people to advance into leadership positions. If you are an outstanding salesperson, it seems only natural that you would be selected to be a sales manager. People in leadership positions are put there because they prove to be good technicians, clinicians, salespersons or promoters. The dilemma is that none of these attributes necessarily qualifies a person to be a great coach or leader. As a matter of fact, it is often the case that the very thing that makes a person a great individual performer, and gets the person promoted, will prove to be their greatest hindrance to becoming a great coach or leader. The ego drive for self-promotion has sounded the death toll for the career of many a manager. The ability to pass credit to another, and even promote them because of their performance skills, is often difficult for top performers.

To be a great coach, you have to take pride in the fact that you helped someone else get her name in the company newsletter. This is what having a servant's heart means.

A desire to help people succeed. Can you imagine anyone *without* a desire to help others succeed, being effective as a coach? I can't. That, in a nutshell, is the *raison d'être*, the reason for being. To be truly effective, the coach should have a burning desire that cannot be quenched until the person being coached has reached the summit of whatever mountain he is climbing. This directed desire to help others achieve success means that the coach's ego must be kept below the surface at all times. Realizing that most coaches did not get to that position by hiding their light under a bushel, this might prove difficult for some. Nevertheless, a coach must keep the person he's coaching uppermost in his consciousness.

Great coaches live to make others successful. Their success is tied to the success of others. Pick any successful athletic coach and, while winning is their ultimate goal, helping individual athletes do their very best, day after day, is what they do. Winning is the icing on the cake, and the coach realizes that winning is usually the natural outcome as each performer is doing their very best.

Great coaches want to see others succeed. They delight in seeing others accomplish more than anyone thought possible. Can you imagine a father that doesn't wish for his son to become more successful than he himself was? Great coaches are like that also. Great athletic coaches were, in many cases, outstanding athletes in their own right. In spite of this, their excitement comes when one member of the team excels at the sport and becomes a household name.

In the corporate world, as in athletics, coaches are selected because they were once successful performers. Sometimes in both athletics and business, the fact that they were outstanding performers can cause some difficulties for them in performing their duties. It could prove difficult to look beyond others' errors, or personal flaws in their players. A great coach, like a great parent, teacher, wife, husband, minister or manager, does not try to make someone into a carbon copy of himself. A great coach helps the person become the best he can be. They do this by beginning with the person where they are, and not where they wish he was. This is a true desire to help people succeed. A great coach is truly, *"The wind beneath the wings"* of another person.

A winning attitude. Can you imagine anyone starting out on a quest with mediocrity in mind?

"I'm heading for the Yukon, and I hope I find just a little bit of gold, maybe enough to pay for my trip."

"I'm heading out to Nepal. We're going to climb Mount Everest. I sure hope we can make it up to the base camp."

"Boy, am I excited. I've just been invited to be a part of the crew of an underwater treasure-seeking vessel. We'll probably be gone at least two months. I hope we find at least one or two pieces of eight on the ocean bottom."

"As a father, I hope that my son is motivated by me to at least graduate from the eighth grade."

"I'm heading out on a quest for the holy grail. I just know we're going to discover some clay pots in those caves. I just know it!"

"With all my heart I want that position as a coach in our company. If you give me the job, I promise to work hard to be mediocre. Thank you a lot, or at least, a little bit."

Of course, no one in her right mind would deliberately set out to be mediocre. And no coach would set out to coach someone towards mediocrity either. In spite of the odds, a great coach is always pushing or pulling others forward, and he does this with a winning attitude. Failure isn't in his vocabulary. A winning attitude means that, in spite of temporary setbacks, a coach is always confident in the final outcome.

Jineane Ford, a news anchor on the NBC affiliate in Phoenix, Arizona, was a contestant in the Miss USA pageant several years ago. Much of Jineane's success in being crowned Miss USA can be attributed not only to her beauty, but also to her attitude, courage, resourcefulness and resilience. While walking up the stairs during the evening gown event of the contest, Jineane caught her gown on her shoe and sprawled face first on the platform. She got up, dusted the front of her dress slowly and deliberately, and as the stunned audience watched, she turned to the judges, smiled, curtsied and continued across the stage with great dignity and style. The audience was totally taken back and amazed at her calmness and ability to overcome this setback. When the finalists were selected, her ability to handle adversity, as well as her stunning beauty, intelligence and undisputed class were rewarded.

Winners sometimes fail, but they are not failures. This is the difference. Some of history's greatest accomplishments were by people who suffered through tremendous failures in their lives. Thomas Edison failed thousands of times to perfect the electric light bulb. He kept each of his attempts on display, perhaps to remind himself and others that can't quit just because you failed at first. He continued until he was successful, and thanks to him, the light in my office is contributing to this book.

The North didn't win every battle in the American Civil War. And Jefferson Davis, president of the Confederacy, was not a failure either, even though the South conceded defeat. Davis was later offered a Senate seat in congress, but he declined the offer.

Can you imagine a salesperson who never fails to make the sale? Can you imagine a corporation never feeling a pinch or experiencing a setback in the market? Can you imagine a coach who never sees his coaching slip into old habits, slide into failure patterns or fall back into negative attitudes once in a while? It is all a part of the process on the path toward success.

When the coach practices a winning attitude *consistently*, there is one more blessing attached to it: it is catching! That's right! It's contagious! When you are in the company of another person who has a winning attitude, you are probably going to pick it up to some degree. Unfortunately, humans are prone to pick up negative attitudes, as well. There is an old saying, "If you laugh, the world laughs with you. If you cry, you cry alone." Don't put too much trust in that old saying. Go to a movie with a sad ending, and look around you at the audience. We call it a tearjerker. Most of the audience is either crying or trying to hold back tears!

Have you ever been to see a movie where the hero comes out on top? People actually applaud at the end! Doesn't that seem strange? No one in the movie, or anyone who worked on the movie, can hear the applause. Who is the applause for? It is for the audience, of course.

The great coach—you for instance—must rise above your own setbacks, difficulties and personal problems to shine forth with a winning attitude. Then everyone can applaud. Circumstances don't *make* you what you are, they *reveal* what you are.

If you think you are beaten, you are.
If you think you dare not, you don't.
If you would like to win, but think that you can't,
Chances are you won't.
If you think you're outclassed, you are.
For out in the world you'll find:
Success begins with a person's will,
It's only a state of mind.
If you think you're a loser, you are.
For out in the world you'll find,
Life's battles don't always go
To the swiftest or strongest man.

But sooner or later, the one who wins,
Is the one who thinks he can.
~ Anonymous

A commitment to excellence. The first sentence in Jim Collins' book *Good to Great*[12] is, "Good is the enemy of great." He goes on to add, "And that is one of the key reasons we have so little that becomes great. We don't have great schools, principally because we have good schools. We don't have great government, principally because we have good government. Few people attain great lives, in large part because it is just so easy to settle for a good life."

Great coaches have more than a commitment to excellence; they are intolerant of anything short of excellence. And they are aware that excellence will only occur when the expectation for excellence is everywhere. This is in daily conversations, product manufacturing, sales and customer relations, management direction and even in the corporate mission statement. It is rare when an individual performs outside the level of expectations provided for them.

It would be strange to hear a professional athlete say, "Well, we lost every game this year, but next year luck will be on our side. We'll play at the same skill level and with the same intensity, but we expect to win the championship." Well, as a wise person once said, "The definition of insanity is doing the same things over and over again and expecting to see different results."

When Jim took over as Vice President of Sales for a software training company, the division for which he was responsible was ranked twenty-seventh in revenue within the company. Within two years they had climbed to the number one spot. One could argue that market factors and other outside influences played some part in this change of fortune. But from day one, Jim set the expectations that his division would become the number one office in the company. And from day one, the entire staff began to act and talk as if they were already number one. Did Jim believe what he taught and coached others to believe? Yes, he did!

In spite of appearances, Jim still believed. Did his staff all believe from day one that they could achieve this distinction? Probably not. If they had believed from the beginning, Jim would not have had to coach at all. He could have merely reclined in his executive chair and contemplated all the success he was going to enjoy. He would not have to apply the whip coming down the home stretch. Jim's commitment to excellence, by his own words and deeds, caused others to follow his lead, think excellence and practice success.

If someone you know has a personal commitment to excellence, a drive to do the very best in all they do, you can be assured they will always be in the top 10%. Why is this? It is because few people have made that commitment to excellence.

Think about this for a moment. If more people in your firm were committed to excellence, what would it mean, in dollars and cents, to your company? I think you understand what I'm suggesting. The stronger the commitment to excellence is, the greater the chance of success. If the coach has it, the players will catch it. That's a law of life. Contagion in this case is a good thing. It will spread and keep on going.

The ability to foster trust. The dictionary definition of trust is, "reliance on the integrity and justice of a person." Trust is the basis for all human relationships. Whether public or private, trust is a necessary ingredient.

Interestingly enough, trust can be built, much like a building can be erected on a vacant lot. On the lot, you begin by clearing out all the weeds, trash and debris left by others. Then you consider the lot to be clean and ready to level. With considerable pre-planning, you construct the foundation, making certain it is strong and fortified. It is made of durable materials that can withstand floods and earthquakes. Next, you build the superstructure. This is also made of quality materials. You check the construction as it progresses. And once the superstructure is complete, it is time to finish the interior. This is where the heart of the building exists. This is where the guests who visit can feel the warmth, the beating heart of the building. This is where beauty and order can be presented. This is where finesse finds its home.

Trust can be built in much the same manner. Before the building of trust can begin, there is some preliminary work to be done. Weeds, trash, and debris have to be cleared out of the relationship. Sometimes this can be a very heavy task.

Many people carry a heavy load, and sometimes they have carried it for a long time. If a coach is trying to build trust, and leftover debris still exists, he might be paying for things he didn't want, dealing with the "baggage."

That reminds me of a plaintive song written and performed by Hank Williams, "Your Cold, Cold Heart." The pertinent line is, *"Another love before my time, made your heart sad and blue, and so my heart is paying now for things I didn't do."*

Sometimes the debris can be cleared with a few questions that are carefully and diplomatically phrased. This is where the communication skills of the great coach come into play. After all, you wouldn't feel comfortable putting in the foundation of your building with all the trash and debris still on the field. After the field is cleared, you have to level it before you can build a foundation of trust.

A key to remember is that you're not an owner talking to a slave. You're not even a boss talking down to an employee. Even the playing field. Swallow your ego. Hide your executive washroom key. Loosen your tie. And don't stand quite so tall and regal when you speak. You cannot build your building of trust from your office. You must build it on the lot. You have to make the journey to the place where you want to build trust.

Now that you have cleared and leveled the field, done your research and planning and discovered as much as you can about the person you are going to coach, you are ready for the foundation. Make certain it is strong, made of durable materials, and make certain to withstand all the psychological storms that come against it.

The hardest part is over. If things have been built effectively up to this point, the superstructure can be erected rather quickly. Even when the interior of beauty and order is finished, and everything is going smoothly with the person you are coaching, be alert to the necessary maintenance.

Think of trust as a bridge between two people. Bridges need constant maintenance. The Brooklyn Bridge was built in the 1800's. Since its construction, the painting of the bridge has never been concluded. As soon as the paint crew reaches one end of the bridge, the process begins all over again. Trust between two people is much the same. Be alert to corrosion that might set in and damage the relationship. Maintenance is a coach's responsibility.

Trust comes from observable, predictable and repeatable behavior. When we can predict how someone will act or react, we can, with some degree of certainty, feel safe with that individual. Trust is largely a function of safety. This is one of the basic needs of human beings.

Debra and Pam were friends. They were friends not only at work, but in their personal life as well. Debra was a manager, moving up in her company. She was forced to make a decision that affected Pam in an adverse way. When Pam confronted Debra, the conversation went something like this: "I thought we were friends. You really put me in a bad way. How can I trust you again?"

Trust is vital for effective relationships to exist. It is imperative for a coach to have trust from the people they coach. They simply won't tell them enough, tell them the truth, or reveal how they really feel about things going on in their lives or on the job. Without this information, a coach cannot do her job.

A coach can be a motivating and corrective force in your organization. You are fortunate if you have professional coaches working for your firm. If you don't, you should encourage those who possess the right skills, desires and attitudes to become coaches for your firm.

Those climbing their way up the corporate ladder, or those who have malfunctioned on the job need help. And keep this in mind: when an employee screws up, he is probably only five per cent bad and ninety-five per cent good. Some people are fired for being only five per cent bad.

Coaching can help save that individual most of the time. A coach can make the difference between success and failure for an individual, a department or perhaps even the corporation itself.

Application of V.A.L.U.E.S. to Coaching

Marcus Bollinger was rather despondent as he sat in his cubicle at Morris & Company, Financial Planners. Marcus had graduated three years earlier with a degree in economics. He felt he had been overlooked at Morris on at least two occasions. Once, when Jeff Jacobs had been transferred to the Philadelphia office, and another time when a person who had no business degree had been promoted to a supervisor position. He really didn't feel good working under someone who had no academic preparation in finance or economics.

Because he felt he had been passed over for promotion, he had cut down on his production and had made a couple of mistakes on customer accounts. Fortunately, Jack Burns, his department chief had caught both of them, so no harm was done. Marcus didn't really think his work cutback was serious, since he had always done more than he should have anyway.

It certainly wasn't anything that could put his job in jeopardy, or was it? Jack had informed Marcus that he was sending around what he called a "corporate coach" to talk to him. "That's just what I need," thought Marcus, "some high-powered, pushy busybody to tell me everything that's wrong with me. They'll probably even tell me what I need to set me straight."

Marlene Drew had only been in the Urbana office for a couple of months. She had been working for Morris for over fourteen years. Her last stint was in Memphis for five years. She was familiar with the company's policies and procedures and was pretty well committed to the firm's mission statement. "To serve every client as if they were our only client." The CEO of the company, Brian Baxter, selected her to fill the newly created position of corporate coach. Marcus was her first assignment. She had briefly glanced at Marcus' personnel records, but had decided she wanted to get a "clean slate" view of him for herself.

"Hello, Marcus, I'm Marlene. Can we talk?"

"Oh, sure, come into my domain and have a seat."

"Thanks. First of all, Marcus, I'm not here to criticize or find fault with you. I hope you understand that."

"Okay."

"From what I hear, you've set some pretty high standards for people to follow since you've been with the company."

"Really? I haven't heard that."

"Well you should have, so I guess I'm the one to tell you."

"Thank you. What does a corporate coach do anyway, Marlene?"

"My job is to visit with people that show great promise and maybe just need a little boost. Sometimes I can also help someone that might be having a problem at work."

"I don't think I've got a big problem."

"Nor do I. I'm just here to ask you a few questions. I'm pretty independent in what I do. I'm only responsible to Brian Baxter, and I don't have to tell him anything I don't want to. That's the agreement I made when I accepted the corporate coach job. And, anything we discuss here, stays here, and that's a promise."

"Really? That's not the Brian I know."

"Well, Morris, let's just call this the new Brian, okay?"

"How do you feel things are going for you right now on your job?"

"Oh, I don't know, okay, I guess."

"Are you happy with the way your career is headed?"

"I'm not sure happy is the word to describe it. I think I've been screwed over a couple of times."

"What do you feel should have happened?"

"I should have been considered for promotion."

"Did you talk with anyone about how you felt and what you expected?"

"No, I thought it was somebody else's job to tell me if I wasn't in the running."

"Where do you feel you would be if you had been promoted? What kind of things would you have that you don't have now?"

"A bigger space, that's for sure."

"What else?"

"More recognition for what I've done. Right now I feel like a piece of trash."

"I think I understand somewhat how you feel, Morris. I'll come back at 2:00 on Tuesday, and we'll look at some things that are possible for you to do to push your career goals a bit higher. If you'd like I can work with you to set some short-term goals, and maybe we can come up with a progress plan that you'll feel good about. Would that be allright with you?"

"Sure, I'll be looking forward to it. Thanks, Marlene."

Marlene greeted Morris by valuing him and presenting a general question, "Can we talk?" She then quickly valued him and explained her presence and her purpose. She presented the relevant question, "How do you feel things are going for you right now on the job?" and she shifted quickly to the expectation questions, "Are you happy with the way your career is headed? What do you feel should have happened?"

Next, she used an advantage question, "What kind of things would you have that you don't have now?" Marlene then moved to explain her offer to help him with some goals and plans for the future. She also used the take-it-to-the-next-level question, "Is that all right with you?"

The coach's job is to bring out the best in an individual and help her solve a problem or move her to a higher level. Marlene certainly began that process with Morris.

Why is coaching needed so badly in the corporate world today? Why now, more than ever before, is there so much stress, so much discord, so many errors being made by employees? Why is so little skill being expressed in the work force? And why are there so few successful training programs being offered to employees?

The answers may be numerous, but certainly the quality of new employees being hired for key positions has to be questioned. It is estimated that over one-third of new hires lack the technical and mathematical skills necessary to fulfill their responsibilities.

Corporate executives claim that most of their problems in their business come as a result of hiring poor-quality workers. A lot of people want jobs, but not enough of them are prepared for the high-tech atmosphere and activities of today's corporate world. This is why corporate coaches are needed. This is why those special individuals who have the servant's heart, a desire to help people succeed, a winning attitude and the ability to foster trust, are so needed in the corporate world.

Today's corporate coach is much like the coach of the Bad News Bears. He has to take a ragamuffin team of misfits and mold them into a team of winners. He has to implant new winning attitudes in the minds of employees who have not experienced much success in the business world. He also has to be a rally master for the team even though maybe they haven't won yet. He has to invest time, effort, energy, skill, motivation and heart in his work with people.

We need coaches to work with people, instead of having the corporation fire them for inefficiency. Consider that an employee who makes a mistake, which gets him fired, is probably 80 to 90 percent efficient on the job. If he is at least not this good, he probably would not have lasted this long. To fire him, replace him, and train someone new, who probably won't be perfect either, costs the company lots of time and money.

A business coach can at least work with the people to save them and the company a lot of misery. A good coach can literally turn people around and produce quality employees out of Bad-News-Bears-type people.

Isn't it really the manager's job to make better people out of the employees? Why can't the manager be the coach?

Oftentimes, the problem with employees is related directly to their manager. A manager is the boss. A manager is the overseer looking for the evil that lurks in the hearts of her employees. She is the punisher, the ramrod, the driver, the force rather than the power. A coach, on the other hand, comes in as a teacher, mentor and counselor. A coach can also act as a guide, a gentle prodder, friend, ally and minister.

A coach is someone to whom you can confide, knowing it will be kept confidential. A coach is someone you can trust, and someone who will give you the benefit of the doubt. He is there to help, not destroy.

There are some specific ways that coaches can communicate with those who have needs. These might be needs centered around learning, so they can move up the ladder of success. Or they might also need to learn ways to overcome their tendency to mess things up on the job. The V.A.L.U.E.S. system of communication can help.

V = Valuing. Because of the sensitivity of the coaching job, and the absolute necessity of fostering trust and confidence with the employee, the valuing step is probably the most important of the six steps of the communication process..

The way a coach approaches the employee is so vital to the success of the business. When the coach greets the employee, the greeting must be filled with caring and friendship. You can work with a supervisor who doesn't love you, and one who lets you know it. You cannot work with a coach who has this same attitude. This is why good coaches are so special and unique. They have to have a genuine love for people and a burning desire to serve.

A coach is like a person I once met. She said that whenever she first met someone she wouldn't let herself see anything about him she didn't like until she first found three things about him she *did* like. It isn't so strange that she had more friends than enemies. Wouldn't you have liked to have your children in her fifth grade classroom?

We've discussed remembering names and how important this is in valuing people. People are unique individuals, and their name helps distinguish that individuality. It sets them apart from others. It's something to call their own. And people like to hear it, especially from someone they trust and respect. Can you imagine your best friend never calling you by your name? You'd probably end up saying something to them about that. When you care enough to know and use a person's name, you are honoring their place in your heart. If you look them in the eye and say, "Hi, John, you're looking good today," you just might make their day.

If you want to know how you really feel about your name, just meet someone face-to-face with the exact name as yours. You'll feel strange, I guarantee it. Inside you might even feel a bit of animosity toward that person. Here is a stranger that has *your* name. He doesn't have your father's name or your uncle's name, instead he has *your* name. How dare he have your name! I think you might want to ask him to change it.

Your first responsibility as a coach is to value the other person and let her know she is important to you and to the organization. Do not ever meet with someone without making a positive comment that lets her know she is valued.

Sometimes the problem the employee is working through is that no one has valued them. This may be true on the job or in their home and social life. When you care enough to value them, you might open doors for the real person inside to come out. One of the most simple, yet profound, truths of human interaction is, if you want people to like and trust you, like and trust them first!

A = Asking. The primary difference between the teacher and the coach is that the teacher *asks* the student what they know. The coach asks the employee what they know *and* how they *feel*.

Asking questions is vital for both jobs. If the student isn't turned around for the better by going to school, the teacher, principal and school board blame the student. If the business coach isn't able to turn the errant employee around, she may be seen as a failure. This makes coaching a tough job, and one that requires total dedication and commitment to the task at hand.

After doing a good job of valuing the person to be coached, the coach then turns to the next step, that of asking effective questions. We can say that they need to ask G.R.E.A.T. Questions©! If you go to the doctor with some ailment, you expect them to ask you the right questions: "What seems to be your trouble, Sam?" "Where does it hurt, Linda?" "How long have you been experiencing pain in your shoulder, Pete?" "Are you presently taking any medications?" "Are you allergic to any drugs?"

You would be upset if, instead of asking you the preceding questions, the doctor asked you, "Who was your prom date in high school?" "Have you gotten those shots for your Dobermans?" "Have you ever been to the Dells in Wisconsin?" "Where do you get your car serviced?" You'd probably say something to the effect of, "Could we get back to my stomach ache, please, Doctor?"

In the same way, the coach has to ask the right questions if they are going to receive the right answers, and discover a need that exists. Without this discovery, it will be difficult to deliver help.

Great coaches have tools that help them diagnose issues that may affect performance. In sales, it may be a pre- or post-call planning form or a sales-call evaluation process. In customer service, it might be feedback from customers or peers. Don't forget to use your G.R.E.A.T. Questions® when planning your coaching session.

You have just moved a good employee into a new position, but he is having trouble meeting his production quota.

Here is an example of a coaching session using G.R.E.A.T. Questions®:

G = General Question: "How are you feeling about your new job, Pete?"

R = Relevant Question: "How are you doing in regards to your production quota?"

E = Expectations Question: "Do you feel that the quotas are reasonable?"

A = Advantage Question: "I know you want to meet your objectives so that you can get your production bonus. Wouldn't it be great if you could meet these objectives?"

T = Take-it-to-the-Next-Level Question: "What specifically do we need to do to help you reach your goals?"

A coach realizes that he needs to ask questions to determine the employee's needs, so he should prepare some G.R.E.A.T. questions ahead of time. Of course, the ways in which the coaching session progresses are partly determined by what further questions need to be asked.

Being prepared is critical! Below are a few coaching questions that can prove helpful.

- "What have you done this week that you are proud of?"

- "What things have you accomplished for which you'd like to receive praise?"

- "Who has benefited the most from your good work this past week?"

- "What would you do if you had unlimited resources?"

- "What would you like to have accomplished but fell a bit short in achieving?"

- "In what ways can I help you achieve what you want to get done?"

- "What do you feel is the best that you can do in your present job?"

- "Where do you see yourself in the company two years from now?"

- "What are the most important things that you believe will contribute to your success here on the job?"

- "What two or three things do you think you can improve on in the next month or so?"

- "I've noticed marked improvement in your work in the past month. What's next on your agenda of improvement?"

Using G.R.E.A.T. Questions® is important for any coach. Without good questions, a coach cannot know where to go next.

L = Listening: Asking good questions is important, but without exercising excellent listening skills, the answers fall on deaf ears. Most communication is about listening. The days of seminar leaders lecturing for hours have passed. Not many participants are willing to sit still for training that does not let them participate verbally in the process of training. A coach does not need to monopolize the time in a coaching session in order to direct the session, since the person asking the questions is in control of the session. In fact, one of a coach's primary functions is to bring the employee out of her shell and get her talking.

As we have already discovered, communication is an activity in which someone is talking and someone is listening. A coach needs to be primarily a listener. Active listening on the part of the coach—total body, mind, and spirit listening—is the coach's responsibility. And when you are involved in active listening, you are using one more method of communicating: you value the person speaking. Your rapt attention says, "You are important to me, and what you have to tell me is important to me, so please continue." In other words, as a part of the listening process, you must ask pertinent questions, so long as they are not perceived as interruptions or put downs.

Listening helps a coach learn things that cannot be discovered in any other way. Sometimes rumors that have been spread through the grapevine can be clarified in a good coaching session. That is, if the coach is a good listener. Sometimes listening effectively can help you hear more than just the words coming your way.

The coach must be an *empathetic* listener. This means that the coach has to listen from the speaker's point of view. The coach has to bury feelings, prejudices, values, beliefs and pre-conceived notions in order to hear the values and beliefs held by the employee.

Empathy, as we have discussed before, requires a great deal from the individual. A good coach has the ability to empathize with anyone. Effectively employed, empathy yields valuable results. And because coaching can result in some confidential information being discussed, make sure you always coach in a private place that is free from noise and interruptions.

U = Understanding: It is the coach's job to either bring an employee closer to their potential so they can move up in the company, or to correct some deficiency in the employee's performance. This is done by getting to know the employee well. It is only through coming to an understanding from the employee's perspective and motivation that a coach can be effective, and this includes the employee's intellectual and emotional intelligence. A coach needs to recognize at what level the employee is able to exercise emotional control, how well the employee understands her own emotional intelligence and how well she enters into social discourse while keeping her emotions bridled. Of course, there are times when a coach might prefer that the employee reveal some emotion if the issues being discussed call for it.

A great coach has to possess a large degree of emotional intelligence. He needs to know who he is, what emotions he possesses, the strength of those emotions, how to control them and what implications this suggests for social and business relationships.

E = Empowering: While valuing people is perhaps the most important job of a business coach, empowering the employees is also a tremendous responsibility.

We must assume that it is a coach's basic function to either raise the employee up to a higher level so he can be promoted and become more effective and valuable to the company, or to correct some malfunction in the employee's performance. In either case, we assume that the employee is somewhat disabled. This means he is disabled in the sense that he is not at the level expected of him or he isn't functioning as well as he could be.

If your car breaks down on the freeway, you would say it was disabled. Your emergency action would be to call AAA or a similar roadside service. The service would come to where you are and empower your vehicle.

Think of the sub-par employee as a vehicle that has broken down on the freeway. A roadside service technician will either do what they can to get the vehicle moving, or they will tow it to a repair shop. As the coach, instead of examining sparkplugs, wires, motor, pistons and the like, you are examining the values, beliefs, motives, expectations and dreams of the employee. The coach is much like a mechanic, using whatever tools available in the her tool kit to empower the person. And just like the disabled automobile, the employee might not be able to identify what's broken or out of place. The coach needs to discover the problem and uncover ways to fix it, including using whatever influence is available to get the company to fix the problem, if appropriate.

Sometimes the best way to empower people is to help them raise their expectations. When people have big dreams, it is quite possible they will reach higher and higher until they get to the top. Helping employees voice their increased expectations is a great way to see how powerful the concept of a "self-fulfilling prophesy" can be. But it starts with a coach helping people see their full capability.

First, a good coach discovers what desires the employees have. Second, she helps them translate those desires into the next step, which is verbalizing an expectation. And third, the coach supports them by making certain they realize the level of faith she has in them and in their ability to do the job.

A coach's real purpose is to act as an agent of change for the person being coached. If there was no reason for the person to change, a coach would not be needed. One of the best ways to get the person to change for the better is to *empower* them. Empowering them gives them the power to do and to be all they can be.

S = Serving: The very definition of coach is "one who serves others." In fact, nothing identifies the great coach any better than to say that they are busy serving. That is what a coaching session is all about—serving someone's needs.

Many times the coach is called upon to hide his light under a bushel, so he can bring out the employee's light.

It is fairly easy to measure the success of a coach. In sports, it is when the team wins. In the family, it is when the children grow up to become good citizens, with good morals, good judgment, good manners and a successful career. In the corporate world, a coach is successful when those he coaches change for the better. He has either raised their level of proficiency, or eliminated errors on the job.

Serving others in need is what the job of coaching entails. Being available, mentally, morally and physically is vital to the success of this very important function within the corporation.

CHAPTER 11

THE POWER OF PERCEPTION

> "Perception is the cruelest form of reality."
> *Anonymous*

I n a classic television series, the comedian Flip Wilson portrayed a character named Josephine. One of Josephine's oft-stated comments was, "What you see is what you get." How very true that statement is for us today. What we see is definitely what we get. For most people, perception **is** reality. And understanding *that* concept is a key for effectively employing the tools presented in this book.

Taking this perception concept to the next step, someone once said, "Perception is the *cruelest* form of reality." Yes, perception can be cruel when it is not true. Have you known people who you felt had the wrong perception of you? It was not fair, but that was their perception, their reality. How we perceive ourselves, our job, our company, our role, our industry, our ability, is our reality.

But there is good news! If the perception is not true, it can be changed! If we perceive ourselves in an unfavorable light, we can change that!

We have already established that we have to value ourselves *before* we can value others. If there are areas in our lives that do not meet our needs, we find ourselves living and performing without passion or enthusiasm in those areas.

In the *Bible*, the book of Proverbs says, "As a man think in his heart, so is he." How we view our internal and external world causes us to respond as we do.

Given this truth, we must consider how we perceive ourselves, our ability, our talents, our potential, our environment, our associations, our position, our family, our industry, our firm, our professional duties, our product or service and our role in all aspects of our life.

If the task of examining our perceptions seems formidable, be assured that it is. And yet, without this first step of self-awareness, we cannot make adjustments and grow in our ability to communicate effectively. Consider the following quotes.

- Marcus Aurelius: "There is no thought but tends to quickly convert itself into energy."

- Buddha: "All that we are is a result of what we have thought."

- William James: "The greatest discovery of our generation is that human beings can alter their lives by altering their state of mind."

- Paul, the Apostle: "Be not conformed to this world, but be ye transformed by the renewing of your mind, …"

In other words, changing how you think can change your very life, and if that change is in a positive direction, it can change your life for the better! The power of our perceptions can raise us to a higher level and can certainly enhance our ability to communicate more effectively.

Perhaps the following example can illustrate this concept. Many years ago in Italy, a visitor from another land was observing three workmen.

> The visitor asked the first man, "Sir, what are you doing?"

The man replied, "It's really none of your business, but I'll tell you anyway. I'm carrying these huge stones, and they're breaking my back. Now get away, and leave me alone."

The visitor asked the second man, "Sir, what are you doing?"

He responded, "Why, I'm carrying these stones so that my family can eat and have a roof over their head. That's what I'm doing."

The tourist then asked the third man, "Sir, what are you doing?"

He said, "I'm building a wall around the courtyard of this cathedral. It is going to be a wonderful place. There will be trees for the birds, and the yard will be full of children playing. It will be the most wonderful place in the city!"

All of these workmen were doing the same job. Which one do you suppose was happiest in his job? Which one had the most satisfying life? A good perception of the job you hold is so important.

On occasion, all of us have to perform tasks and make decisions that are not enjoyable or fulfilling. In looking at your job description, are the requirements of your work stimulating and fulfilling? Are you able to commit to those tasks every day with enthusiasm? If you answer no, then you may find yourself spending more time trying to get out of doing them than you spend in fulfilling your responsibilities. A customer service representative was once overheard to say, "I would love my job if I didn't have to deal with customers." Now that is someone who has missed the point!

Many influences affect the way in which you fulfill your work tasks. Let's examine a few.

Perception of yourself

How you see yourself, your satisfaction with your life, your personal achievements thus far, and your progression toward your life's goals are vital to your success day by day. Volumes are written on self-esteem and the effect it has on our ability to function.

Many of us have been lucky enough to have someone in our lives who saw more in us than we saw in ourselves. That person helped us expand our perception of ourselves, and we grew because of it.

Tim Sullivan was one such person. He was the manager of a large, successful residential real estate office with new people joining the firm every day. Outside of his office, there was a board that had the sales agents' names, their monthly production, and year-to-date sales totals. The names were ranked by yearly production. And yet, the Number One spot was always left open.

When Tim hired a new person, he placed their magnetic nametag at the bottom of the board. He then asked the new hire to go to the board and take his or her nameplate from the bottom of the board and place it in the Number One spot. He then put his hand on the rookie's shoulder and together they stood there and looked at the Number One spot for several minutes.

Tim then asked the rookie, "What do you think of your name being in the Number One spot? How does it feel? I know you can do it, but how long do you think it will take you to earn that spot? What do we have to do today to get you started?"

Tim was changing that new employee's perspective from that of a rookie to a Number One producer in the office. He was tremendously successful for many years. He is retired now, but people still stop by to see Tim and thank him. After all these years, they say they can still see their name at the top of the board.

Perception of your ability

As Manager of Training for a major insurance company, it was part of my job to conduct an assessment of each trainee who participated in our sales training program. This three-week intensive training was designed to give the future agents the product knowledge and sales methods necessary for their success. It also was designed to show them what it meant to build a career in the insurance business.

One of my jobs was to attempt to discern their potential for success as agents. I tested the participants to determine their level of intellectual mastery of the materials presented, but in a classroom environment I was unable to test their inner drive and determination, the qualities they needed to propel them toward their potential.

One of my students named Bob was a prime example of my inability to measure future success potential. Before noon on the first day of the training, the other class members were rolling their eyes every time Bob spoke. He had this grating personality that was matched with a lack of the most basic information needed for success in the insurance industry. One of the first statements he made to the class was that he intended to become the number one salesperson on the team.

After the first day of class, I called his manager and suggested to him that he should be concerned about Bob. I felt that he could become an embarrassment to both the manager and the company. I shared with him how, in the middle of a discussion on how to rate a homeowner's policy, Bob raised his hand and asked, "How often do you pay an annual premium?"

Bob's manager agreed with me and immediately began

formulating a plan that was sure to move Bob out of his office, and hopefully, out of the industry within a short period of time.

The work plan Bob's manager designed for him was nearly impossible, and it included a requirement for sales completed with an activity level far beyond one that was reasonable.

I kept in touch and was amazed that Bob, not knowing he was set up to fail, met all of his manager's objectives. He arrived at 6:30 every morning. He planned his day and was out the door an hour later. He worked all day, most days without taking a lunch break, and ended his appointments around 8:00 every night. After a year in the field, Bob was at the top of his team's performance.

Looking back on my experience with Bob, it is now clear to me that I could not see in the classroom what it was that was driving Bob to perform. He saw himself as a winner and he was willing to do whatever it took to be successful. Perception creates ego drive and ego drive is the power source that drives the engine of success.

Perception of your industry

Recently while consulting with a pharmaceutical company, I met a young woman. She had tears in her eyes as she told me that she was not going home for the Thanksgiving holiday like she did every year. Apparently every time she went home for the holidays where her family was gathered, she became the object of ridicule because of her sales position in the pharmaceutical industry. Members of her family had suffered because of the high cost of prescriptions, and they felt that their situation was the result of greed in the pharmaceutical firms. This woman was having a hard time committing to the activities of her job the way she should, because the disgruntled members of her family had influenced her perception of her industry.

Instead of seeing her job as providing healthful and useful products to assist physicians in their job, she was suffering from the negativity she received at family gatherings, and she was now endorsing her family's beliefs, although not totally consciously.

How we see our industry can have a major impact upon our ability to function at the highest level.

Perception of your company

"I could never work for that company, their reputation is terrible." That phrase spells doom and failure. In spite of this, many people work for companies or organizations that do not meet their basic expectations. Can you, or anyone else, who has no respect for a company, commit to the activities that it takes to be successful? If you are embarrassed, or ashamed of your company you probably will not be able to perform to your potential in any role.

Perception of your product or service

Have you known people who have been asked to represent a product or service that they felt was inferior or substandard? Over the long term, we will not violate our conscience. If we work for a firm that provides inferior products or services, we will come to believe that this is a direct reflection on ourselves. We will feel guilty and will not be able to fulfill our job responsibilities.

I heard a man tell a personal story about his daughter when she was younger. He told how when she was 2 years old, she was the victim of an abusive baby sitter. The baby sitter shook her, slapped her and threw her against the wall. As a result, the girl had brain damage that resulted in her having dozens of seizures a day. The doctors felt she would never be able to live a normal life.

Enter this "miracle drug" that prevents seizures. As a result of this drug, his teenage daughter is living an almost normal life. She had not had a seizure in over 12 years.

Do you feel that this person could have done an exceptional job representing this product and company to physicians? Not only was he motivated to help others in his situation, but also his belief in his product would have been a strong driving force in his motivation to be successful.

If you do not have an attachment to the service you provide, the product you sell or the people you lead or a heart to serve the people you coach, you will not have the passion to generate the energy to be successful.

Perception of your role

Do you see your role in your firm as one of value? Do you see yourself empowered, respected and able to use your talents and abilities? If not, you will find yourself being filled with resentment. If your ideas are regularly rejected and your resources not provided, and if there is not a support system for you, you will find it difficult to be committed or engaged productively in your job. We all want to feel like we have meaningful work and that we can be a part of an organization that values and respects our contributions.

If you agree that our perceptions are largely responsible for our responses to people and situations, and if you believe that it is possible to change your perceptions, then perhaps you might consider making some changes in your own life and work.

It takes 21-31 days to make or break a habit. Consider how you and your organization would be affected if, for the next 21 days, everyone with whom you and others in your organization you came in contact, was made to feel valued.

You asked great questions, listened empathically, empowered and empowered them to perform at their maximum potential and served. Do you think it might be a transforming experience?

Happiness, joy, contentment and success are matters of the heart, not of circumstance. We all are unique and have the potential to achieve great and wonderful things. Sometimes, like a dormant rose, those wonderful qualities are lying somewhere inside us, waiting for the warm sunshine of another person to tell us that we have great potential. Someone who sees more in us than we see in ourselves. Someone who recognizes and helps awaken the greatness that is all of us. Someone who helps us change our perception of who we are and what we can accomplish.

The Rose

It is the face of faith I see,
In every flower, every tree.
Although their shroud is winter's snow,
Calm, serene, their hearts beat slow.
What faith, what dreams cause them to bear
The sunless days with patience rare?
I asked a rose, "Are you alive?
The winter's long, can you survive?
The rose spoke softly in my ear,
"I live, and know and have no fear.
You've asked my secret, I'll confide,
My strength and will lies deep inside."

—Jim Mayfield —

CHAPTER 12

COMMUNICATING WITH V.A.L.U.E.S.

Instead of summing up the book in a traditional manner, I have chosen to use a different strategy by selecting key points from each chapter. These key points can serve you and others in your company as discussion starters for leadership and coaching.

1. Introduction

2. Communication is an art and a science.

3. Communication is a process.

4. For relationships, communication must happen.

5. For commerce, communication must happen.

6. A seamless process of communication, spanning all departments, is possible and profitable.

7. The purpose of communication is to open the door for exchange of thought.

Chapter 1: Valuing

1. C. K. Chesterton: "How much larger your life would be if your self were smaller in it, if you could really look at other people with common curiosity and pleasure."

2. C. K. Chesterton: "Love means loving the unlovable—or it is no virtue at all."

3. The first step in loving is to know what you are loving.

4. Our values precede our beliefs, and our beliefs cause our actions.

5. John Donne: "All mankind is of one author, and is one volume. Any man's death diminishes me, because I am involved in mankind."

6. Heroic deeds occur because somebody values somebody.

7. Albert Einstein: "Man's purpose on earth is to serve mankind."

8. The responsibility of all of us, regardless of our role, is on serving others.

9. It doesn't take much effort to value people.

10. There is nothing you can do that is more noble, more powerful or more honoring, than to value someone.

Chapter 2: Asking

1. David R. Hawkins: "Slight errors in the formation of questions result in gross errors in the answers that follow."

2. It is a leader's function to bring about the best in his or her employees.

3. In the business environment, questions serve a most important purpose—to enhance communication.

4. Asking questions is a great way to learn about anything you do not already know.

5. The essence of intelligence is the ability to ask good questions.

6. Use the G.R.E.A.T. Questions® technique.

7. Keep questions positive and focused on the issues or problems at hand.

Chapter 3: Listening

1. The quality of a person's life can be largely equated with the quality of their listening.

2. Forty-five percent of our communicative day is spent listening.

3. Effective listening has to be learned and is teachable.

4. In the corporate world, much of our success is related to how well we listen.

5. Listening is both intellectual and emotional.

6. Effective listening takes effort.

7. Barriers can keep us from excelling at listening.

8. Active listening is present when the listener is totally involved in the communication process.

9. Empathetic listeners listen for understanding, because they care about people.

10. Listening can help you win friends and influence people.

11. President Calvin Coolidge: "No one ever listened himself out of a job."

12. Listening helps you build trust, confidence and rapport.

13. Listening can help you in your own career.

Chapter 4: Understanding

1. Communication is a one-to-one exchange.

2. To understand another person, it is helpful to know their learning style and their behavior style.

3. A person is a mix of styles, but has one dominant style.

4. Behavior styles dictate a person's actions.

5. Intellectual intelligence used to be the exclusive measure of success.

6. Emotional intelligence is now a better precursor of success than is intellectual intelligence.

7. The person who has all the answers is infected with the "disease of allness."

8. Both intellectual and emotional intelligence can be learned.

9. Those who have made the commitment to empathize with others report amazing changes in their lives.

Chapter 5: Empowering

1. To empower someone is to give them power, means or ability. It is to make them competent, authorize them or make things easy.

2. Great expectations have given us the standard of living we enjoy today.

3. Lack comes largely as the result of weak expectations.

4. "Hold Backs" are those things in life that hold us back from becoming what we can become.

5. Expectations are what drive us all.

6. A person tends to become precisely what he or she expects to become.

7. Setting great expectations is a powerful way to make things happen.

8. Higher expectations find their basis in the successes we enjoy.

9. Robert Browning: "Man's reach should exceed his grasp, or what's a heaven for?"

10. Ask not what someone can do for you; ask what you can do for them.

11. Do not promise anyone the world. Help them win it by empowering them.

Chapter 6: Serving

1. We are all leaders of one kind or another.

2. As leaders it is our privilege and responsibility to serve our followers.

3. To find our people's needs, you must look beyond your own biases.

4. Needs and wants are not the same.

5. You may have to put your own needs on hold to meet the needs of others.

6. The effective leader is one who discovers and meets the needs of others to achieve some purpose that provides benefit.

7. The effective leader is one who serves others.

Chapter 7: Leadership with V.A.L.U.E.S.

1. A leader is an agent of change.

2. A leader sees situations from all angles.

3. An individual cannot be a leader without followers.

4. Tom Peters and Robert Waterman: "Treat people as adults. Treat them with dignity, treat them with respect."

5. Leaders must be held accountable for their actions.

6. To be effective, a leader must become a fount of knowledge.

7. A leader must know people.

8. A leader must be a master of communication.

9. A leader needs to remember people's names.

10. Marcus Buckingham and Curt Coffman: "People leave managers, not companies."

11. A leader needs to be emotionally intelligent.

12. One of the most important functions for a leader is to empower others.

13. A leader finds needs and fills them.

Chapter 8: Selling Behavior change with V.A.L.U.E.S

1. Convincing someone to change is a complicated, difficult task.

2. V.A.L.U.E.S. is an effective Motivational Interviewing tool.

3. Being a Correctional Professional has more to do with internal characteristics, such as attitude than skills of influence and research.

4. Getting someone to change an attitude or behavior is much the same as trying to sell someone a product or idea.

5. When a client trusts, believes and respects you, and understands that you have their best interest at heart, he or she will be more responsive to you.

6. A Correctional Professional needs a dedicated work ethic and persistence.

7. A Correctional Professional needs to be a lifelong learner.

8. Planning and having a set of outcome measures is critical for the successful Correctional Professional.

Chapter 9: Customer Service with V.A.L.U.E.S.

1. A company will spend 100 million dollars on advertising and turn down a request from a customer for $25.00.

2. It costs as much as five times more to get a new customer than to keep an old one.

3. People buy because of customer service.

4. Companies hire the most inexperienced applicants for customer service representatives.

5. Customer service representatives are often relegated to second-class status.

6. Many customer service representatives have little authority to make adjustments.

7. Customer service is often separated from the rest of the firm.

8. It is rare for the entire work force to be trained in customer service.

9. Each employee's job depends on good customer service.

10. Reward people for good customer service actions.

11. Robert Desatnick: "Employee relations equal customer relations. The two are inseparable."

12. Employees who are not trained in customer service run rampant in our society.

13. "How may I help you?" is a great way to start helping a customer.

14. The customer service representative is a problem solver.

15. The customer service representative needs to empower the customer.

Chapter 10: Coaching with V.A.L.U.E.S.

1. A coach's job is to help someone grow from mediocrity to greatness.

2. A coach's success is assured when someone grows.

3. Coaches are found in every profession.

4. Coaches have been around since man appeared on the earth.

5. Great coaches have these five traits: a servant's heart, a desire to help people succeed, a winning attitude, a commitment to excellence and the ability to foster trust.

6. Kahlil Gibran: "The teacher…gives not of his wisdom, but rather leads you to the threshold of your own mind."

7. Galileo Galilei: "You cannot teach a man anything. You can only help him discover it within himself."

8. The coach must be a servant.

9. The coach has to plant new winning attitudes in the minds of employees.

10. The coach has to be a rally master.

11. Instead of firing sub-par employees, companies need to assign coaches to work with them.

12. The coach is there to help, not destroy.

13. The coach's primary job is to value people.

14. The coach needs a high degree of emotional intelligence.

15. The real purpose of the coach is to act as an agent of change for the person being coached.

16. Last, but not least, the coach must be a servant.

Chapter 11: The Power of Perception

1. We have to value ourselves before we can value others.

2. William James: "The greatest discovery of our generation is that human beings can alter their lives by altering their state of mind."

3. Perception of your job – limits or fosters success.

4. Perception of yourself – limits or fosters success.

5. Perception of your ability – limits or fosters success.

6. Perception of your industry – limits or fosters success.

7. Perception of your company – limits or fosters success.

8. Perception of your product or service – limits or fosters success.

9. Perception of your role – limits or fosters success.

10. Simple changes of mind can affect your life now.

11. The greatest deterrent to creativity is habit.

12. Jim Mayfield: "You've asked my secret, I'll confide, my strength and will lies deep inside."

We hope that you have found value in *Communicating with V.A.L.U.E.S.* It is part philosophy, part experience, part skills and part common sense. We believe that individuals and corporations can utilize this seamless approach to communication to help empower people to reach their potential.

READING LIST FOR
PERSONAL GROWTH AND POWER

The Bible
Power vs. Force, David R. Hawkins
As A Man Thinketh, James Allen
Dare to be Yourself, Alan Cohen
You Can't Afford the Luxury of a Negative Thought,
        John Roger and Peter McWilliams
Fire in the Soul, Joan Borysenko
The Greatest Salesman in the World, Og Mandino
The Prophet, Kahlil Gibran
The Power of Your Subconscious Mind, Dr. Joseph Murray
Influence, Robert B. Cialdini
The Inner Game of Golf, Timothy Galwey
The Inner Game of Tennis, Timothy Galwey
Love Is Letting Go of Fear, Gerald Jampolsky, M. D.
One Person Can Make a Difference, Gerald Jampolsky, M. D.
The Magic of Believing, Claude Bristol
Manifest Your Destiny, Wayne Dyer
The Richest Man in Babylon, George Clason
Real Magic, Wayne Dyer
Real Power, Janet Hagberg
The Road Less Traveled, M. Scott Peck
The Seven Habits of Highly Effective People, Stephen R. Covey
Simple Abundance, Sarah Ban Breathnach
Think and Grow Rich, Napoleon Hill
No Boundary, Ken Wilbur
Visualization for Change, Patrick Fanning
I'm OK - You're OK, Thomas A. Harris, M. D.
Applied Imagination, Alex Osborn
Expectations and Possibilities, Joe Batten
Learned Optimism, Martin E. P. Seligman, Ph. D.
The Artist's Way, A Spiritual Path to Higher Creativity, Julia Cameron
See You at the Top, Zig Ziglar
The Neuropsychology of Creativity, William C. Miller
The You That Could Be, Dr. Fitzhugh Dodson
Celebrate Yourself, Dorothy Corkille Briggs

Jonathan Livingston Seagull, Richard Bach
Awaken to Your Spiritual Self, M. J. Abadie
Your Erroneous Zones, Wayne Dyer
Pulling Your Own Strings, Wayne Dyer
Your Word is Your Wand, Florence Scovel Shinn
The Knight in Rusty Armor, Robert Fisher
The Aladdin Factor, Jack Canfield and Mark Victor Hansen
Take Charge, Success Tactics for Business and Life, Joan Koob Cannie
Frogs Into Princes, Neuro Linguistic Programming,
    Richard Bandler and John Grinder
Games People Play, The Handbook of Transactional Analysis,
    Eric Berne, M. D.
Dare To Win, Jack Canfield and Mark Victor Hansen
Unconditional Life, Discovering the Power to Fulfill Your Dreams,
    Deepak Chopra, M. D.
Quantum Healing, Deepak Chopra, M. D.
Psycho-Cybernetics, Maxwell Maltz
Primal Leadership: Realizing the Power of Emotional Intelligence,
    Daniel Goleman, Annie McKee and Richard Boyatzis

FOOTNOTES

[1] *Influence: Science and Practice*, Allyn & Bacon, 2001

[2] *QBQ! The Question Behind the Question*, Denver Press, 2001

[3] Use by permission – *The Universal Language;*
a reference manual by Bill Bonnstetter and Judy Suiter, TTI 2004

[4] *Working With Emotional Intelligence*, Bantam Book, 1998

[5] *Mind Power into the 21st Century*, Zoetic Books, 2001

[6] *Business and Its Beliefs* McGraw-Hill, 1963

[7] *In Search of Excellence*, Warner Books, 1982

[8] *First Break All The Rules: What the World's Greatest Managers Do Differently*,
Simon & Schuster, 1999

[10] *How I Raised Myself from Failure to Success in Selling*, Prentice Hall Publishers, 1986

[11] *Patient Satisfaction, Defining, Measuring, and Improving the Experience of Care*,
Health Administration Press, 2003

[12] *Good To Great*, Harper Collins Publishing, 2001

James Young is Vice President of Training and Development for The Williams Institute for Ethics Management. As an author and speaker, James travels internationally delivering presentations and training in the areas of ethics, customer service, coaching and leadership. He has two sons, Dan and Ryan and a grandson Vaden. James enjoys writing, reading, hiking and playing his guitar.

Jim Mayfield, Ph.D., grew up on a farm in Indiana. He dropped out of high school at age 15 to join the Merchant Marine during World War II. When he was 28 years old he realized that greater things lay ahead of him, so he took the GED Exam and entered the University. Six years later he earned his Ph.D. Degree from Michigan State University in Speech/Communication. For over 40 years, Jim has served as a professor, minister, counselor and seeker of truth.

For information about training classes for your organization on V.A.L.U.E.S. Selling©, V.A.L.U.E.S. Customer Service©, V.A.L.U.E.S. Coaching©, V.A.L.U.E.S. Leadership©, contact:

TWI Publishing
Scottsdale, Arizona
480-517-1891
info@ethics-twi.org
www.ethics-twi.org